D0415302

DIARMUID GAVIN

homefront in the garden

DIARMUID GAVIN

homefront in the garden

Inspirational designs and ideas
from the cutting-edge BBC TV series

Photography by Jonathan Buckley

To Jack and Joan Gavin, who have always given love

This book is published to accompany the television series *Home Front in the Garden* which is produced by the BBC.

Executive producer: Rachel Innes-Lumsden
Series producer: Dan Adamson

Published by BBC Worldwide Ltd, Woodlands,
80 Wood Lane, London W12 0TT

First published 2001
Reprinted 2001
This paperback edition published 2002
Text copyright © Diarmuid Gavin 2001
The moral right of the author has been asserted
Photographs copyright © Jonathan Buckley 2001

All rights reserved. No part of this book may be reproduced in any form or by any means, without the permission in writing from the publisher, except by a reviewer who may quote brief passages in a review.

ISBN: 0 563 53479 6

Commissioning Editor: Nicky Copeland
Project Editor: Helena Caldon
Cover Art Direction: Pene Parker
Book Art Direction: Lisa Pettibone
Book Design: Isobel Gillan and John Calvert
Illustrations: Ann Ramsbottom

Set in Minion and DIN Mittelshrift
Printed and bound in Great Britain by Butler & Tanner Ltd, Frome & London
Colour separations by Radstock Reproductions, Midsomer Norton
Cover printed by Belmont Press Ltd., Northampton

ACKNOWLEDGEMENTS

To work on *Home Front in the Garden* is exhilarating. I've always done the plans and the gardening but over the years a great team have created the programme.

Thanks to Sean and Paul Cunningham who have worked miracles over the years. Pure genius.

Rachel Innes-Lumsden who is inspirational and the best. Dan Adamson who knows what it is all about and grew with it. Franny Moyle who is a bright shining light. Simon Shaw, Daisy Goodwin, Kim Evans and Ana Lloyd who started it all off. Jane Root who is a believer and a promoter. Nicky Copeland for love, brilliance and patience. John Noel, Polly Hill, Nik Linen and all at John Noel Management for everything. Stuart Sharpless for interpreting and finding solutions, Neil Pike for plants from day one, Tessa Shaw and Anne McKevitt.

At the BBC:

My first book was a long process, especially for Nicky Copeland – thanks for sticking with it over the years. Helena Caldon – wow, so that's how books happen. Alison Reynolds – thanks for the kick start. Jonathan Buckley, brilliant photographer, and Isobel Gillan for her wonderful design work.

Thanks to Seamus Geoghegan, Julie Savill, Adam Pascoe and all at the website beeb.com.

Every programme we make is a massive undertaking. Through the efforts of many, though, it has not become a production line.

Directors: Dan Adamson, Lucy Hooper, Andy Devonshire, Helen Foulkes, Dave Smith, Ed Bazalgette, Randall Wright, James Strong, Orla Doherty, Paul Tucker, Amelia Dare, Pattie Steeples.

Production team: Cynthia Charles, Hanna Wesson, Seb Illis, Tessa Carey, Paul Middleton, Eden Palm, Sue Banks, Judi Wild-Howe, Zoe Ingham, Deborah Harry, John Lister, Jonathan Hallam, Dominic Brandon, Jonty Sale, Gordon Whistance, Jonathan Hassid, Betty Wallace, Lorraine Shea, Richard Cane, Barbara Gibson, Charles Pominion, John Briner.

Garden builders over the years:
Liam Barron, Rob Green, Dave Eaves, Gareth Nixon, Damon Brawn, Enrique Casado, Paolo Goncalves, Drew, Oliver Knowles, Jay, Tony Gardener, Branton Bramford, Colin.

Without whose help we're nobody:
Barry Storey, Dean and Jason Harvey, Bill Bray, David Rosewarne, Geoff Allen, Robin Riseley, Paula Al Lach, Dom Greyer, Derek Draper, Adrian Gibbs, Dermot McDermot, Jonny Dobbyn and all at Rolawn, Tendercare Nurseries, Civic Trees, Luxcrete, Marshalls, Timber Decking Association, Dulux, Charles Morris Topsoil, Potter and Soar, Preedy Glass, Lynch's Plant Hire, Speedy Hire, Travis Perkins.

And in Ireland thanks to:
Vincent Barnes, Tom Curran, Wendy O'Conghaile, Bernard O'Rourke, Sally Hanna, Rose Doherty, Barry Cotter, Sean Keighran, the Botanic Gardens, Glasnevin, and remembering my friend Eamon Ferry. Love to Declan, Niamh and Emer Gavin. Love to Terry, Ronan, Yayee, Jane and Karl, Timothy, Madeleine and the kids. My English family are: Pat, Jane, Eilish, Rory, Niall and the Mannings in Liverpool.

And finally, to my writing partner, who is also my beautiful wife, Justine.

CONTENTS

FOREWORD

I was brought up in the suburbs of Dublin, Ireland's capital city. Living anywhere in Ireland you were always surrounded by green. The fabled forty shades, long celebrated in song, are no exaggeration and, to a degree, neither is the rain. But it's a good climate, at times damp and at times resembling the tropics. As a youngster I didn't realise that technically it was a temperate climate. In effect, this means a lack of extremes, wet or dry, hot or cold. The result of being brushed by the warm Gulf Stream is a lack of frost in many parts of the country, so it was not unusual to see an abundance of plants such as cordylines, hebes and eucalyptus surrounding you. On holidays in coastal regions you'd see exotics like the Tasmanian tree fern, *Dicksonia antarctica*, self-seeding in the shade of their parents. The hedgerows of Cork, Kerry and Donegal were often awash for what seemed like hundreds of miles with fuchsia and montbretia. With the added effect of global warming, which in recent memory has led to a lack of winters as we used to know them, Ireland, believe it or not, is growing greener.

But when I was growing up gardening was never taken that seriously. There was a healthy tradition and maybe even an Irish gardening style, but in general gardening was for the pleasure of large estate owners or fanatics who seemed to be members of secret societies. They still exist. But now gardening has emerged as a profession and a hobby; and it is a pastime that has been embraced with vigorous enthusiasm. There are many reasons for this – society is becoming more affluent, home ownership is increasing, people are having more leisure time and, of course, television and glossy magazines have an influence. So I arrived at garden design at a fortuitous time.

From 1985 to 1988 I spent three happy years studying horticulture at the National Botanic Gardens in Dublin. Like every other student, I was geared towards the more traditional aspect of garden design because, I suppose, we were unaware of any other choices available. This is the thing that really got me both frustrated and excited. I realised that unless I made an effort to do something different, my career as a garden designer would be more about creating 'lovely' gardens and maintaining a small business – the emphasis would be on keeping an eye on the bank balance to make sure I remained solvent. But I wanted my emphasis to be on having the freedom to push outdoor design forwards. I spent some years developing gardens throughout Ireland, but unfortunately the all-important client did not share my enthusiasm for things new. There were good times and tough times but in the mid-nineties a sense of adventure led me to the Chelsea Flower Show with two gardens. The first, in 1994, was a very romantic traditional garden designed to please the Royal Horticultural Society; the second a vibrant city garden designed to please me.

Between the jigs and the reels, I ended up creating gardens for television and over the next few years it was as though a dam had burst and many ideas that had been fermenting made their way on to the small screen. These ideas come at the oddest of times, but they stay in my mind until the ins and outs of their construction, their budget, their aesthetic appeal and their maintenance have been fully worked out.

I get my ideas from everywhere. My experiences in life are not restricted to gardening ones and certainly in my youth the idea of being a gardener or garden designer was not foremost in my mind. But I have always been fascinated by design in all its forms, whether that be clothes design, architecture, art or the pop video during its heyday in the eighties. Dublin, too, has been in a state of constant change which has affected its architecture, gardens and people. Over the last fifteen years it has been transformed from a purely commercial city centre, empty at weekends, to a vibrant living and working community. All these things have a strong influence on my outlook.

A garden doesn't have to have wild or unexpected twists to excite me. Planting is foremost – whether set out by a designer or arrived at over the years in a haphazard manner. I've been learning about gardening for a long time and that journey has led me through a period of creating in a variety of styles. Some have been beautiful, some have been bland. The lack of a market for the more progressive ideas led to a personal stagnation for some years and it is only now through *Home Front in the Garden* that I feel that I am back learning. It has been a fascinating experience exploring the use of some new materials, colours and plants in a more subtle and yet challenging way, a combination of suburban, traditional and modern. It is these ideas together with my passion for plants that I bring to you in this book.

INTRODUCTION

LIGHTING

PLANTING

LAWNS

DECKING

WATER

LIVING SPACE

PLAY AREAS

STORAGE

BUILDINGS

A BRIEF HISTORY OF GARDEN DESIGN

The desire to create a garden is an innate human trait which stems from two basic considerations – food production and aesthetic gratification. The ability of a garden to produce, seduce, educate and entertain has always been known. Gardens, by their very nature, are artificial creations. We should never lose sight of this – they consist of man imposing his control over land, plant and sometimes creature. Gardens are necessary for human existence. To some Westerners, however, gardens have become high fashion. This has sometimes led to a misunderstanding of or disregard for their origins and functions and therefore, I think, to a dissolution of their potential joys. There is a risk that gardens have become fashion accessories. Maybe there is no harm in this as it causes people to be inventive, but my fear is that a lack of understanding of how garden styles have developed and of their basic function can lead to a reverence for the style itself with no real substance. For some people, the joy of the garden is lost through a monstrous snobbery, an obsession with certain periods or plant collections, but now it's being wrestled free for the common man. Gardening has been democratised. So, if we cast aside the shackles of snobby and conservative associations and take a brief look at the history of design, we can see how styles have arrived for both true and fashionable reasons and then go forward.

All great ancient civilisations – including the Roman, Chinese, Japanese, Greek, Egyptian and Persian – created garden styles that have been handed down to us. But they weren't necessarily created as styles in the modern sense of fashion – gardens were originally made primarily for functional use. These functional uses developed in ornate styles as a reaction to the landscape – often a taming of the land. I always take as my start in garden history the Persian king who decided he wanted to be able to hunt wild animals all year round, so he built walls to enclose vast tracts of land then planted trees and shrubs. Here a desire for sport led to the evolution of a garden style. In fact, the Persian word for garden was 'paradeiza' – Paradise. In ancient Babylonia, a king whose territory consisted of very flat, boring plains married a girl who was from somewhere very hilly. She was heartbroken and homesick – she loved her guy but felt she lived in an alien place. So he created an artificial mountain for her, which we now know as the Hanging Gardens of Babylon – one of the seven great wonders of the ancient world. Hollow clay brick columns supported terraces bursting with lush green growth. The inside of these columns was filled with soil so that trees with deep root systems could establish freely and an innovative irrigation system was invented. Then there is the Italian terrace garden developed from a simple desire to create flat usable spaces out of hilly terrain; and the Japanese were always great at taking somebody else's original idea and making it even better. Their gardens, originally inspired by the Chinese, reflect a deeply spiritual nation and their creation of miniature landscapes show their reverence for nature. The tea ceremony, the arched bridge and the pagodas are deeply embedded in their social, cultural and religious life. It is extraordinary that the essence of the Japanese garden is often available in a 'Disney-fied' version from your garden centre or as a bonsai in a cardboard box from Marks and Spencer.

Garden design in the third millennium has developed a need to subdivide the garden into areas for play, plants and recreation.

Rather than be a slave to construction materials which have been handed down to us historically, we now have the ability to use modern manufacturing processes to create structures and details which are of our time.

A number of garden styles have historically been refined or developed in Britain. Monarchs of different kingdoms like to impress each other and an English ruler could get madly jealous if a French counterpart was putting together great displays of wealth, power, horticultural expertise and imagination to reshape and reinvent their patch. Keeping up with the Joneses isn't a modern phenomenon. The English cottage garden style, while apparently being working class, never really was as we imagine it. Believe me, one of its pioneers, Gertrude Jekyll, wasn't exactly poor, and neither were her clients. But it is a style that's fixed in our head, and one that owes plenty to romantic notions and chocolate-box paintings. In reality, the true cottage garden might have more in common with today's allotment. In his excellent books and videos about cottage gardens, the late Geoff Hamilton talks about the reality of this form.

Recently garden design has moved to the suburbs. When I think of growing up with gardens, I have visions of this 'Terry and June, Tom and Barbara' existence culminating with the social-climbing Hyacinth Bouquet. It's an amazing thought that our neat front gardens of this period are still being exported. In the film *American Beauty* we see Annette Bening, kitted out in matching gardening clogs and gloves, manicuring her perfect front rose garden.

Nostalgia in all its forms is a massive industry and gardening doesn't escape it. How much of this is a desire to retreat to a time when we think we were happy, either individually or as a nation? While there are great merits in the current fashion for accurately restoring historical gardens, we should be careful about developing gardening by numbers and just copying past gardening styles. Why create restoration dramas to adorn mock-Georgian houses? Of course, you must have gathered by now that I am the greatest gardening snob of them all. But, side by side, I also believe that everybody should have the freedom to do what they want. I know this is a contradiction.

Historically gardens have always been developed by the rich. In Britain, gardens were created by those wealthy enough to travel to far-off lands and bring back never-before-seen plants and ornamentation, which were then displayed at their palaces or public places such as Kew Gardens. Gardening hasn't always been the passion of the common man in this country, and certainly not garden design, and yet today gardening is said to be sexy, the new rock 'n' roll. This green revolution has occurred, I believe, because of a number of factors.

Firstly, as a result of the huge increase in home ownership, more people than ever before have gardens. However, many of us feel the styles that have been passed down over the generations may not be suited to our own ways of using a garden, so we have begun to want to explore the possibilities of our small plots. Today we have more leisure time and more disposable income and, as with many other areas in our lives, we want something new and unusual to reflect their uniqueness.

Another factor which has influenced the way we see our gardens is that, while we may not have the climate of California or Sydney, we've spent years watching people on television who live in those places enjoy their outside spaces and this has tempted us beyond the back door more than ever before. Coupled with this, architecture itself has radically changed, and now that many of us live in

Dramatic new ways are now being used to divide communal areas from private ones.

increasingly small boxes, we tend to indulge our passion for light and for creating views by using a lot of glass in our home construction. This use of glass, along with the demise of the net curtain, means we now view our plots all year round.

Growing up, I lived in a typical semi-detached house in suburbia. Running across the back of the house, beyond the kitchen door, was a five-foot strip of concrete. And leading down the garden, following the washing line, was a rough concrete pathway, which ended up at the door of the bicycle shed. How was that for imagination? On our road, nearly every garden was the same, with the occasional vegetable patch belonging to the more green-fingered type.

And then came the double-glazing salesman, who turned out to be a hugely important influence in garden design! Where slick sales patter was involved, my mum was a softie and in no time at all a crowd of workmen had replaced the rackety wood windows with new double glazing. At the back of the house the walls seemed to have turned to glass. New double doors led to the outside and all of a sudden we became aware of the garden. Previously it had been easy to shut it away from sight, but now it begged attention. We became aware of the amount of space available, another area of the house that should be used. Its time as a football pitch was over and it lay neglected.

So what has happened is that we have begun to use our gardens all year round, in one way or another. Even when the weather does not allow for permanent sunbathing, the garden is entertaining, a fascinating type of ever-changing show to be viewed, appreciated and indulged in. A new generation of gardeners, prompted by designers

The relationship between garden buildings and the house is blurred in this arch building. You decide whether it's half-greenhouse, half-summerhouse, or just a sleek exterior bedroom allowing you to gaze up at the stars as you lie surrounded by trees.

such as John Brookes, have been encouraged to view their gardens as living spaces or outside rooms. These are over-used terms but it doesn't mean that they are not valid. It may seem sacrilege to picture the plants as adornments to an exterior space, but for me the term opens up radical possibilities. If we live in suburbia or cities, enclosed spaces are what we are used to and often the amount of land given over for a garden area is small. Very few people would hesitate to design or even just 'do up' a room in their house. But garden design seems to frustrate the majority of the population even though, in effect, you are just taking control of the available outdoor space you have and making it work for you.

Events such as the Chelsea Flower Show and the Hampton Court Flower Show have begun to promote fashionable gardening styles just as the couture houses of Paris and Milan have for decades been influencing what we wear. Alongside this, garden designers have been looking for ways of creating new exciting statements. The desires of the innovative and the traditional converge at gardening events where planting fashions and the constraints of traditional materials are exposed and contemporary or unusual materials are showcased. We are still experimenting with the new and some of these materials and techniques will become classics, while others will fall by the wayside and be seen as passing fads.

Not very long ago, if you had wanted to employ a garden designer who could be labelled as contemporary rather than traditional, the search would have been quite an ordeal. But now, since gardening has become so fashionable, they're ten a penny. But be careful – what is required from this new breed of designers is an innate understanding of gardens and how they work, form and function and of the science of horticulture. The worst thing to do is to create something just for the sake of it. Many garden designs suffer from a veneer of modernity but don't have an idea of the way in which plants work together to create a stimulating environment. Modern doesn't mean carving everything into spiral shapes or chucking around a whole load of crushed gravel or galvanised containers.

HOME FRONT ETHOS: THE OUTDOOR ROOM

Home Front in the Garden originated as a spin-off of the *Home Front* television programme where design excitement was fully explored and the boundaries in terms of colour, material, function and creativity were pushed to their limits. It is well known that interior design became incredibly adventurous during the nineties. *Home Front in the Garden* aims to do the same, taking new ideas, new colours, new materials and, most of all, new enthusiasm outdoors.

Many people are scared of gardens. They don't know what to do. Our mission is to demystify the design process and yet make it exciting. So, rather than fearing that, once designed, your garden will be an unmanageable jungle, we aim to show you how to take control using new and innovative ideas.

Most new houses have gardens that people consider to be very small, but if you look at it in another way they are often the biggest space you will have available to you in your home. The programme sees the garden as an outdoor room with potential for many uses depending on your lifestyle – relaxing, eating, playing, entertaining, making love. It's not only for growing plants, unless that's your particular passion.

It's very interesting to observe people's reactions when asked about decorating a room in a house as opposed to planning materials for constructing an exterior space. If a person was taken from the street and asked to design a living room, they would make a good stab at it. They would know the choices available for flooring. Their suggestions for consideration would include wooden floors, carpet, tiles, lino or matting. For the walls they would suggest wallpaper, paint, wood panelling or even fabric. They would instantly tell you how many people would be using the room and what type of furniture was needed. Would it be a sofa or individual chairs? What style of furniture do they like? What ornamentation pleases them? Would they have prints, posters or original paintings on the wall? Would the lighting be from the centre of the room or from secondary lamps?

But in the garden it is all too easy to feel stumped. We don't fully consider the materials available to us, how suitable they are for the job in hand and whether they are liked or disliked. There's a tendency to go to the local garden centre or DIY superstore and just make a selection from their limited choice. *Home Front in the Garden* is designed to tackle this dilemma. You don't have to be a plant expert to create or enjoy a garden – have confidence, think laterally and, above all, have fun.

An outdoor stove provides late evening and winter warmth for entertaining all year round.

A raised wooden deck
in this family garden means
the parents can watch the
children play safely on
the sail-covered sandy play
area below.

FORM AND FUNCTION

What I hope we have shown on *Home Front in the Garden* is that when you are designing a garden there are some real practical responsibilities involved. It is pointless, for example, creating a spectacular glass cube suspended over water if the owner cannot maintain or have some way of cleaning it. It is all very well making a sunken area for entertaining and partying, but if you don't put in sump pumps, the area will be flooded under several feet of water at the first sight of rain. All these things show that you may have to compromise where necessary – make sure that the garden you, or the designer, have constructed is capable of being maintained and, most importantly, will last. I am not into throwaway gardens. Unlike interiors that can change with every passing fad with a new lick of paint, I believe that garden features should last for years. The plants themselves do enough changing throughout the seasons and one part of the enduring thrill of gardening in northern Europe is to retreat indoors during the winter months and to rediscover your garden in the spring.

ABOUT THIS BOOK

I hope this book will make you think about your garden or the garden you would like to have some day. It will help you evaluate what a garden is and what a garden means to you on an intellectual and emotional level. In Chapter 1, I look at what you need in your garden functionally and what you would love to have in your garden. It is possible to combine the two successfully. Chapter 2 takes a fresh look at design – which, of course, is always subjective. What is good design? What is bad design? What are the classical designs? What are the basic principles? Where do you get inspiration from? And how can you explore the potential of colour, material and planting?

In Chapter 3 I get back to basics – soil, aspect, climate – and show you how to measure up your garden and put your plan on paper. I also look at practical considerations such as improving your soil, project planning, budgeting, neighbours, and working with garden designers and contractors.

Chapter 4 is based around boundaries – real or visual, which delineate the borders of gardens, or internal boundaries, which subdivide them. In Chapter 5 the options for flooring, a main part of hard landscaping, are examined, ranging from traditional to modern. Chapter 6 looks at the myriad ways in which water can be used in the garden, from fountains to canals. Chapter 7 goes shopping for accessories – furniture, lighting, music – that can add magic to your garden.

In Chapter 8 the real magic arrives. Here I look at the process of developing a planting scheme. How do you acquire the different groups of plants you need for a fulfilling garden? And there's a list of some of my favourites for your consideration.

Finally, all this information is put into context with a selection of case studies of designs for real people's gardens. These demonstrate how to tackle some of the more common problems you might encounter when designing your garden.

Materials such as concrete and metal which have not previously been considered traditional in a garden, are now being used in new and innovative ways.

A QUESTION OF CHOICE

LIGHTING

PLANTING

LAWNS

DECKING

WATER

LIVING SPACE

PLAY AREAS

STORAGE

BUILDINGS

Before you begin to plan your garden, or before you consider asking a designer to help you, take time to think about what you really need and what you'd really love. It's good to take control and to clarify in your own mind exactly what you want from your garden. On the other hand, this isn't the only way. You mightn't have to do this if you have a basic understanding of what you want. Or you mightn't want to do it, preferring to go with the flow and learn by your mistakes. Most good gardeners learn the hard way, which can also be the fun way.

For years the process of my designing gardens for clients was the same. Typically, someone would ring me up and invite me to their home for an initial visit. It would probably be a Saturday morning and have involved a single person, couple or family. After looking at the garden, we would sit around the kitchen table and, over the course of an hour or two, have endless cups of tea. The client would begin by explaining that they wanted a new garden because the space they had wasn't fulfilling their needs, but they didn't know why, and they had some vague questions or suggestions. They would tell me that they would love a beautiful garden but didn't know where to start, what would be in it or how much they should spend on it. Despite this, I always found that by the end of that first meeting, after some gentle (or vigorous) probing, they had unknowingly told me exactly what they did and didn't want. Driving away, I always had a smile on my face because we had arrived at the solution. I felt like Sherlock Holmes, weeding their requirements and desires. Elementary.

Physically writing things down is of enormous help when deciding on the design of your garden.

Make two separate lists headed 'what you require' and 'what you desire'. The first should contain all your needs to suit your lifestyle. The second should be a real wish-list. Don't worry about marrying up the two yet. Everyone's list will be different – you may, for example, have children but no pets, or you may have a cat but really want a fish pond. Whatever your requirements and desires, this chapter shows you what type of things you should take into consideration.

What do you require?

There's absolutely no point in creating a heavenly Zen-type garden with gorgeous rock formations, three-hundred-year-old bonsai Japanese maples and swirls raked into granite sand if you have a golden retriever, a five-year-old boy, and two bicycles which need storage space. So to create a working garden you must first be aware of the practical issues involved. Most people's practical requirements will be different from their neighbours', and at the earliest stage of planning you have to consider what yours are or what they are likely to be. Some of the needs are obvious – maybe as simple as a garden shed, a place to store the bins or a washing line. Others won't be so obvious. A lawn, for instance, could be a much more practical solution than a gravelled surface if you have children.

So at the very start of the planning process think about what your garden will be used for, who will be using it and when they will be using it. Take into consideration how much time you will spend actually gardening and how much time you will spend enjoying the garden. Remember, however,

Strips of turf frame grey concrete slabs and soften an otherwise traditional paved patio area.

REQUIREMENTS CHECKLIST

Low- or high-maintenance garden

Eating or sitting-out area

Pathway through garden

Shed or storage space

Hiding ugly features

Privacy

Noise reduction

Outdoor lighting

Water supply

Play area for children

Somewhere for pets

Washing line

Dustbins

Safety

A raised decking seat has been created underneath an old tree where parents can relax while keeping a watchful eye on the children as they play in their copper pyramid dens.

that low-maintenance gardens are all very well, but some of the most boring gardens I have ever seen are the ones that require little or no maintenance. It is important to strike a healthy balance and to create a garden that works for you.

LOW- OR HIGH-MAINTENANCE GARDEN

How much time do you have to spend tending a garden? Will gardening be a chore or a hobby? It is possible to have low-maintenance gardens or even virtually no-maintenance gardens, but to my mind they can lack soul. Looking after a garden should be fun. On the other hand, you don't want to become a slave to your plot. Whichever you decide, be honest with yourself.

EATING OR SITTING-OUT AREA

Most people will need a dry level area, such as a patio area or deck, to use as a base within a garden. This should ideally be big enough to accommodate the garden furniture you choose, whether that is a single deckchair or a full dining set of table and chairs. Often the requirement for this place is that it is in a warm, sunny position at the different times when the garden is being used. Do you want to sit out in the dusky shade with a glass of wine smelling sweetly-scented stocks, or do you need somewhere where the whole family and friends can swarm around for a barbecue? It may be that more than one area is needed, but whichever you decide, access to the place or places should be good.

PATHWAY THROUGH THE GARDEN

Access will be needed to all areas of the garden that are to be used on a regular basis. This access should be of a dry and non-slippery material. A pathway can also help lead one's eye around the garden, even if the owner doesn't physically venture from the house. But often there is the danger that a pathway can dominate a plan. By its very nature a pathway is a strong line and form – it will often be made from a hard landscape material such as brick, cobble or stone. Think about it carefully – let it link your garden together but don't let it dominate it. This will become obvious as you begin to draw your plan. Also remember not to let your pathway clash with your other main lines, such as your areas laid out for lawn or borders.

RAISED BEDS

If your mobility or eyesight is impaired, take steps at an early stage to discover what type of garden structures are suitable for you. Raised beds are often an excellent way to garden at waist or wheelchair height. Ramps rather than steps or stairs may be an appropriate way of dealing with changes in levels. Make sure you provide plenty of seating throughout the garden.

A SHED OR STORAGE SPACE

Gardens are only really successful if they work on a few different levels. They should please and stimulate all your senses but they should also be functional. That means practical considerations such as: where do you store your spades, forks and shovels; and where do the wheelbarrow and lawnmower go? New houses generally don't contain storage space for gardening paraphernalia, so make provision for a shed in your garden. But fit it in sympathetically – choose a style that will not be at odds with the rest of the garden and be an eyesore. Painting a shed a very dark green will instantly help to tone it down and fade it into the background. Black is also an excellent colour for this. I don't recommend highlighting the shed with a bright colour unless it is extremely pretty. By 'pretty' I probably mean something that has leaded diamond windows, planting troughs for geraniums and a hook for a hanging basket!

HIDING UGLY FEATURES

Is there a blot on your landscape? As a general point, people often draw more attention to structures such as ugly oil tanks by encasing them

A garden seat by Finn Stone is both sculptural and functional in this setting.

Access to a private area can be kept intriguingly secret. In this garden the owner was furnished with her own surfboard bridge which she laid down to cross the pond into her secret garden.

Lights set into the slope were inspired by windows from an aeroplane, and create drama in the garden at night.

in elaborate cages of trellis. This often only highlights the offending but functional feature. If you are using trellis or any other structure, keep it as simple and as well built as possible and establish some climbing plants or wall shrubs against it straightaway. Or, as mentioned already, choose colours which will help to tone it down.

PRIVACY

We're a funny old bunch really. We seem to be locked into a notion that despite the fact that most of us live in communities, we want to spend much of our time creating walls and barriers, strongly defining our personal plots and keeping people out. Tabloid newspapers and sensationalist television programmes love the Leyland cypress wars that cost householders their lifetime savings in court cases. So what are we trying to hide? Most of us actually live quite boring lives. Unless you are the Queen, Madonna or Robbie Williams, I'm afraid people just aren't all that interested in what you get up to in your garden. And even if they are, your version of the Berlin Wall isn't going to stop

them because you can now buy aerial pictures of any piece of land in Britain over the Internet, which are taken by satellites that criss-cross your plot every hour.

So short of putting a roof on your garden, there's no way to shut everyone out. There are other ways of creating privacy within your garden without necessarily erecting barricades – you can excavate downwards, for example. Personally, I am a firm believer in a sense of community and I think there's something quite reassuring about being out in your garden in a row of terraces and seeing everyone else mowing their lawns on a Sunday afternoon.

NOISE REDUCTION

If you live near a motorway, or indeed a school which deposits hundreds of screaming kids into its yard at various break times during the day, you may want to plan for some noise reduction. This can be achieved to some degree by planting relatively tall specimen trees or shrubs or by creating another focus of noise in your own garden such as a dancing fountain.

OUTDOOR LIGHTING

If you will be using your garden mainly in the evening, you may want to think about installing some form of outdoor lighting. This can perform both practical and decorative functions. Lighting can transform a garden into a very different, magical place by night. It can also play a part in security, leaving no dark places for unwanted intruders to hide in.

WATER SUPPLY

Rather than carting bucketfuls of water through your house, it can be good at the earliest stage to have a plumber install an outdoor tap. This can also help if you later want to set up an automatic irrigation system to water your pots or heavy drinkers in the garden when you are on holiday.

A PLAY AREA FOR CHILDREN

A garden may have many different lifetimes. Sometimes it may be needed as not much more than a football pitch. But things needn't stay the same – you may long for a pond yet feel it's too dangerous with a young family, so perhaps it could start life as a sandpit and become a pond when the children are older. Before you make elaborate plans, remember that the garden is a space that should appeal to all members of a family. If you have young children, or young children will be using the space, their interests should be stimulated. They need to play in a safe habitat, often in full view of the house, and therefore planting and other garden features should be planned in conjunction with a degree of safety awareness.

SOMEWHERE FOR PETS

Fido or Bugs Bunny will need a kennel or hutch. Again, they should not dominate the garden – they should fit in well with the overall design. Before you decide where they should be positioned, think about how much access you will give the animal to the garden as a whole and whether a new puppy and massive investment in a landscaped garden would really be such a good idea.

THE WASHING LINE

Hardly a glamorous item, but for a lot of people, especially families with children, this is a major requirement. A washing line should be sited in an open space with good air circulation and excellent access. But it doesn't have to dominate the view from the house. And there are different types available, so you do have a choice. Popular at the moment are swirly lines that are collapsible when not in use and those that retract into a container screwed to a wall. Try to site the line close to the house so that the journey from the back door to the drying clothes is as short a dash as possible in a sudden rainstorm.

DUSTBINS

Dustbins are also necessary in all households. Again they need to be sited near the back door. A recent innovation for wheelie bins is a plastic sleeve that can disguise these necessary containers as a giant busy lizzie or as a carpet of leaves!

SAFETY

Safety is always an important consideration – a dangerous garden is not a relaxing one. But there's no reason for a garden to be hazardous; you just need to be aware of any potential risks – for example, water features around young children, slippery pathways – and design accordingly.

What do you desire?

Desire is much less quantifiable than requirements – it's all about dreaming. Go through the process and don't be disillusioned if, inevitably, some of your desires may need to be redefined later when considering finance, space, planning and even changes to your personal situation.

This is your time to dream, and you should do it over a long period rather than rush straight in. So relax for a while and let the grass grow under your feet! If anything were possible, what would your ultimate garden be like? What would it feel like? Even how would it smell? It can be quite confusing to make a decision when faced with so much choice. In recent years, since gardens became 'trendy', we have been deluged with all sorts of images of the 'ultimate' garden. It is very tempting to just copy something you have seen or rush straight out with your measuring tape, but take time to think about what you really like and dislike.

Gardens, like people, go through several changes over the span of their lives. Indeed, many gardens will have infinite lives. Some gardens will last hundreds of years and obviously will be cared for by many different types of people. Over time, everything changes, whether that be the natural landscape, buildings or fashion styles. The natural evolution in a garden is faster than any other because it is dependent on the forces of nature. A typical person these days may have a strong relationship with three or four gardens over the course of their life. And one's relationship with the concept of a garden over a lifetime is never constant. When I am designing for a client, they often refer to gardens in their past, ones that they grew up in, and make reference to features or plants within these gardens.

So how do you start making your wish-list? Over a period of time, gather together as many articles or pictures from magazines as you can.

Watch all the garden programmes possible and make excuses to snoop around friends' plots. Become a garden tourist. You don't need to be a plant enthusiast to do this – gardens do provide an irresistible joy, whether it is because of their form, colours, sweet scent or air of tranquillity. When you visit different gardens, take a notebook along and jot down what you like and what you don't: features, plants, colour schemes and anything else that catches your eye. It will be invaluable later on.

Your inspiration could be idyllic – perhaps you dream of swinging gently in a hammock surrounded by tropical plants. Or it could be purely horticultural – an urge to grow a blue poppy, for instance. The important thing is to note it. The garden you are planning must work for you on as many levels as possible. But at this stage, forget practicalities. Close your eyes and imagine possibilities.

As you begin to think about your desires, listen to me for a moment. We are tied to tradition and we are also tied to what the neighbours will think. Put both of these thoughts at some distance just for a while. Some things that you would regard as a luxury might enhance your life immeasurably. So

An artist's retreat, set away from the house on green oak stilts set into a large pond, is the perfect getaway.

Television and movie projections and even music in the garden can be celebrated and get you out of a stuffy house on a summer's evening.

are they not worth considering? It is not that long ago that outdoor heaters seemed an absurd notion, but they're not. Over the last few years they have become a big part of sidewalk café culture and now, all of a sudden, domestic versions are for sale in the garden centre. The change is happening that fast. A hot tub set into a deck and screened by black-stemmed bamboos or even a privet hedge could be excellent. In Britain, the pleasure to be derived from a hot soak on a cold winter's day in your garden is incalculable. If it came down to a choice between running a car in a city centre or having an outdoor hot tub, I know which I'd go for. Let the neighbours laugh as the steam rises over their standard roses while you relax in your garden bath, inhaling the scent of real jasmine, stroking the leaves of lavender or crushing a piece of rosemary. But your ideas don't have to be so fantastical; you might want to be able to plug in your computer terminal outside on a hot

day – not really radical, but maybe very appealing.

Consider all the options before dismissing them. Football matches and Formula One races drag people out of the garden – maybe they should drag people into the garden. A television set in the garden is not a sin, I promise you. It might not be traditional, but it may be what you want. Some years ago the rock group U2 criss-crossed the world with a mammoth stadium show called *Zoo TV*. On either side of the stage were two huge television screens, often beaming out at 100,000 people, as lead singer Bono switched channels with his zapper. Those flickering images of countless satellite stations remain in my mind. Television images change every few seconds so, as a light source or a visual installation, a television screen buried in a border could be fascinating. Without sound! Some of these ideas will need imagination and skill to be developed in a functional and safe way. But why not?

THE POWER OF IMAGINATION

Years ago, I was reminded how inspiring the imagination can be while I was driving from one job to another, feeling hassled and fed up with mud and hardcore. Stopping off at a drive-through restaurant, I switched on the radio and was desperately excited to drop in on what seemed to be a new garden being revealed on BBC Radio 4. I quickly picked up the fact that garden designer Paul Cooper had been let loose on the garden of the host. She'd obviously been packed away while he worked his magic and together their voices conveyed the excitement of an owner visiting her newly landscaped plot for the first time. And what a plot – bamboos rustled with the aid of an exterior fan; a stark overpowering wall had been converted into a vertical garden which you could actually climb through; another blank wall had an image of an English country garden beamed on to it by means of a projector; two moving metal spheres created meeting ripples in a still pond; and finally an outdoor bed for some 'adult' enjoyment was discovered at the back of the garden where it couldn't be overlooked by inquisitive neighbours. As the duo progressed through the exciting site, various recordings were triggered such as exotic bird song or an aria by Mozart. This was perfect and because it was radio you were left to create the pictures. Real imagination was at work.

Well, I'm afraid it was real imagination, because the sting in the tail was that it had been a media exercise and all the sounds were courtesy of the BBC's Special Effects Department. But listening without the pictures had made it real for me. And although it never existed in reality I can see that garden in my mind as clearly as any real garden that I have ever visited. Years later, when teaching garden design, I used to turn off the lights, pull the curtains and play the tape to the students. I took as much joy in their reaction to the garden and the realisation of the power of imagination.

Sadly, I can't play you that tape, but I hope that this story illustrates just how important the imagination is in the design process.

By now you should be getting an idea of what you want in your garden. You may even have two lists – one of things that you need and one (probably shorter) of your fantasies. Combining these lists will result in a successful and pleasing garden. But before you reach this stage (see Chapter 3, Back to Basics), contemplate your overall design.

Even in mid-winter, a hot tub can be a joy indeed. The absurdity of outdoor bathing in March can enhance the excitement.

A FRESH LOOK AT DESIGN

LIGHTING

PLANTING

LAWNS

DECKING

WATER

LIVING SPACE

PLAY AREAS

STORAGE

BUILDINGS

Brutal concrete more reminiscent of inner-city tower blocks and stainless steel from industrial kitchens have escaped to enhance garden structures and buildings.

Before you start to design your garden or brief a garden designer using your list of requirements and desires, it's worth having a quick think about the design itself and how you can incorporate into it new sources of inspiration and colours, plants and materials to further the potential of your garden.

New inspiration

Until the 1990s, many people's idea of what a garden should look like was inspired by the classical gardens seen at National Trust properties. Every weekend the family would pile into the car and see what was on offer. And there is nothing wrong with that, as a lot can be learnt from these classical English gardens. It is a silly person who rejects everything that has gone before in a gallop to innovate. For example, in Sissinghurst the idea of breaking up the garden into outdoor rooms, while not being purely original, is certainly carried out to wonderful effect. This can be directly translated to your own plot if, for instance, you have a long, narrow garden that stretches away from the house and doesn't feel comfortable. By breaking it up into smaller rooms, all of a sudden the individual spaces start to make more sense. Similarly, the famous White Garden has inspired people all over the country to create their own mini version of a garden of single colour planting and it is really a forerunner to much contemporary planting.

But there are so many other sources through which your garden design can be inspired. I am often asked where I get the inspiration for my gardens and whether you have to have that certain eye or whether it is something that anyone can

learn. The answer is that I think anyone can be a good designer. Throughout the eighties and nineties we have become much more conscious of design and are developing an awareness akin to other northern European populations, such as the Swedes and the Danes. This has come about simply because there is more money around and marketing has manufactured a demand for products as well as creating an awareness of inherent design qualities. Sometimes this stifles our personal creativity as we allow others to fashion a look for us. We have become used to buying our lifestyle rather than imagining and creating it – you can go down to Ikea and buy an object, a room or now even a whole house off the shelf. The herd mentality is somewhat depressing, but the huge number of people who flock to such stores is also encouraging as it shows that the awareness of good design has significantly increased.

In the eighties there was a fashion for wrap-around sunglasses, one which came directly from the ski slopes. The same shape had for some long time been used on Porsche cars but I had never seen it translated into gardens. That was until I became aware of Charles Jencks's garden in Scotland. I was amazed at his curved grassy mounds, which some time later I noticed had surfaced again in Teletubby land. When I did eventually meet the man himself, I couldn't understand where he was coming from – which was actually some faraway mathematical planet – nonetheless this translation of shape from one field of design to another was not lost on me. However, after my meeting with him I realised with much regret that Mr Jencks didn't even know who Tinky Winky was.

Far from the Taj Mahal, but this suburban garden takes lessons from the masterpiece of symmetry.

CONTEMPORARY DESIGN INFLUENCES

Bang & Olufsen

The Le Corbusier couch

Norman Foster

Ikea

Terence Conran

Bilbao Guggenheim

Marco Pierre White

SMEG

Nike

Spice Girls

Doc Martens

Philip Treacy hats

Philippe Starck

Glass bricks

The Aga

Stainless steel

Paul Smith

Porsche

Zoo TV

City parks

DESIGN INFLUENCES

The designs I have been surrounded by or aware of over the last twenty years come from all parts of life – initially through pop music videos and latterly through gardens, architecture, furnishings, fashion and food.

So look to your design influences in all areas of your life and through them you can create a garden which truly reflects your personality and desires and which will be as original as Charles Jencks's garden. When looking for inspiration be aware that the whole world is full of design. Everything you see and do from the moment you wake up is influenced by it: the look of your bathroom, the labels on your clothes, food preparation in your kitchen, transport to work, the lay-out of offices and even your leisure world have all been touched by design. We are continually bombarded with images and messages through television, music, books, video games, computers and newspapers. And through these images, our likes and dislikes are formed; indeed we are unconsciously constantly deciding which products most reflect our lifestyles, aspirations and image. So open your eyes to the possibility of reflecting the joys and appreciation of loved objects in your garden. Examine exactly what it is that you like about them, whether it's the shapes, the colours, the texture or ease of function, and see how you can capture these qualities in your garden. For example, observing the shape of a loved feature – perhaps the soft curves of a favourite pebble – may lead you to translate that shape directly or inspirationally from the object to your overall plan – say, into an elliptical lawn area rather than just a curved or straight one. To paraphrase William Morris, whom the garden designer

Gertrude Jekyll so admired: 'Never have anything in your home that you don't find beautiful.'

Whilst inspiration can spring from a conscious appreciation of certain objects that you want to reflect in your garden, sometimes ideas just appear from nowhere. This was the case when, in one of my most controversial gardens, I devised a huge steel shark's fin initially as a way of dividing a space and to give the owner some privacy. It was certainly not inspired by the client's love of fish – that would have been a theme garden. But the client did appreciate design and shapes and form, so it was up to me to interpret her wackiness and make a judgement on what she'd like in a garden. Beyond the partition was her own private space, the fin acting as a sort of shield. The engineering factory that made it ended up producing a much more beautiful or brutal piece, depending on how you look at it, than I had initially planned. They took what I had seen as a two-dimensional flat curved wall and created something striking from it. I am not suggesting that everyone goes and has a shark's fin made – but it is an example of creating something totally unique to the owner and of an effective coupling of form and function. Rather than choosing a conventional garden divider like trellis, think laterally. You may need to find your own metaphorical shark's fin.

There is choice out there – you needn't necessarily look to the same old sources of the garden centres and DIY stores or have the same as everyone else. You can go to an engineering firm and ask them to make something unusual for you, or to a woodworker or a blacksmith or a potter. Indeed, if more of us did this there would be fewer chain stores and more of our towns and cities would have individual characteristics.

New planting

Planting is usually an integral part of a garden, but once again times are changing. Don't just be controlled by what is available at the garden centre: make a statement with what you choose to plant. It should tell a story about you as much as any other part of the garden.

For me, inspiration for planting starts off being memory associated – more so than any other aspect of design. Memory of colour, scent or the people associated with gardens and plants in the past plays a very important part. Your choices of plants can come as a reaction to the traditional and what you grew up with or a feeling of wanting to recreate some distant memory you have at the back of your mind. On the road where I lived, the gardens were laid out with lawns and borders and 'pretty' trees. These were species such as flowering cherries and crabs which took an annual prominence as a backdrop to photographs of ourselves, friends and neighbours for holy communions and confirmations. Lawns were kept perfect, colour was added with bedding plants, rows of alyssum, lobelia, alyssum, lobelia. Blue and white borders of bedding vied with the prized campanula and aubrieta. These are memories waiting to be explored, a kind of folk art in the garden because they never go away.

Trends have developed for different types of planting styles. At the moment grasses are extremely fashionable. This is nothing new, but again it is probably the first time that these trends have been enjoyed by the person on the street. Many reviewers are scathing about this new type of gardening – gardening as a fashion – but it has

A traditional herbaceous border would have looked odd with this contemporary backdrop. However, this lush planting helps to unify the garden.

always been that way. The Victorian plant hunters and, indeed, the Dutch bulb traders were forerunners in having their plants of the moment, but never before have plant fashions filtered down to the high street.

Television programmes can also be sources of inspiration – and not just gardening programmes. When the starship *Enterprise* beamed everybody down to some weird and distant planet, they always ended up being surrounded by crazy plants with dramatic leaves. This fuelled my desire to use bolder, more exciting plants. Be open to a planting world beyond herbaceous borders. Take inspiration from anything that appeals to you – meadows, places visited abroad, shapes, patterns and ideas.

In this part of northern Europe, we are incredibly lucky to have a temperate climate and not too many extremes of hot or cold. What it means for plants is that loads of them are happy to grow and do our bidding. However, we tend to rely heavily on a few hundred different species – it's almost like gardening by numbers – and even if a person has never had a relationship with their garden, they will certainly recognise thirty or forty plants. Maybe this is fine, but be aware of the possibilities of different species in terms of their individual beauty and of the ways in which they can be used. I look in detail at some of these specimen plants in Chapter 8 – Designer Plants (pages 116-41).

New colour

Let colour form the background to your creative outpourings. When it comes to colour in the garden, most people think of the chocolate box scenes of the English cottage garden with its herbaceous borders containing the full artist's palette of colours spread out, sympathetically melting into each other. The search for colour perfection goes on – and not only with plants. Today colour in the garden takes on a new dimension as wider ranges of paints become available for wood, stone and metal surfaces. Don't be scared of colour in your garden; even though there has been a huge aversion to using anything other than natural colours as a garden backdrop, I believe it is time to think of colour in different ways. It is time to explore the unlimited and year-round pleasure of colour in all its forms – be it through plants, materials or paint.

Attitudes do seem to be changing – the very fact that there has been a profusion of colours specifically developed for outdoor use by the paint and varnish companies, and that we are no longer restricted just to creosote or varnish, does indicate that things are on the move. However, the manufacturers have still not successfully managed to create a range of tones that are exuberant enough for the outdoors – personally I think they are too bright and garish and not rich enough. It's like painting your garden in toy-town colours. Paint manufacturers hold television programmes partly responsible for their booming business. It seems gardens up and down the country are being painted sky blue and trellis work purple – this is encouraging, but perhaps also needs some caution. Background colour used badly can be brash, self-conscious and attention-seeking: fine if that's the effect you want to go for, but to most people a garden is a place of retreat and escape. Colour should add drama or even subtlety yet not dominate the scene or steal the show.

We shouldn't be scared of colour – it's too much of a cop-out to be subdued and sedate in gardens all the time. Consider all the options before dismissing them.

Cobalt blue tiles provide a dramatic background for plants to perform against. But be careful to use it only where you want the structure to create a strong impact.

The most important thing is to have a co-ordinated approach otherwise you will create what may look like an explosion in a paint factory. To begin with, consider all the surrounding surfaces and plants. Gardens in Britain are generally quite small and you often get a complete view of the garden from the house, so if you concentrate on using one unifying colour, you will rarely go wrong. The rule is – less is more. One of the lessons I learnt very early on in designing gardens is that colour – no matter how subdued or dramatic – will only work well in relation to planting. Plants will tone everything down and more often than not are enhanced by being seen against a vivid background, rather than just against a brick wall.

Background colour can be a brilliant way to disguise those ugly features most gardens have – say, an unattractive shed or outhouse. Colour can also help unite a garden by linking all walls and fences together. So take your time – consider the effect you want to achieve and then proceed with gusto. Finally, I am not advocating painting everything in sight and agree that painting some things, particularly those made from natural materials, can be sacrilegious. Rather than rush in and paint a brick or stone wall, think about it first.

GARDEN COLOURS

White

If people can't think of a colour scheme for interiors, they often end up with white. But white outdoors can be a disaster. In bright sunshine it can look fantastic, but how often does that happen in our climate? It just looks too cold and unwelcoming. As we enter the new millennium it is the colour in vogue in contemporary gardens, but I predict practicality will overtake styling desires and it will soon be replaced. Black will be the new white.

Blue

I am a great fan of blue in the garden in its richer or darker shades. It almost always looks great against green. Cobalt blue is particularly good.

Purple

Similarly, this is a good colour for the garden, particularly dark aubergine.

Red

Personally I rarely use red – it is drama for the sake of drama. The Japanese use it to great effect on archways and bridges, but only as a highlight. Plants can sometimes have a hard time fighting against it.

Brown

As a colour in the garden, brown is generally a no-no because it provides no contrast. That said, brown can look really elegant if used on garden furniture or to disguise ugly features.

Pink

This is a colour to be used judiciously. A deep pink can be very rewarding in brilliant sunlight and creates a Florida Art Deco appearance. I would never use it as an overall colour but rather as a single square or rectangular block. Despite worries of its being too girly, whenever I have used it, it has received universal approval (this really means that even the boys liked it!).

Gold

Very definitely a camp colour, although it is gaining popularity with the current vogue for Moroccan- or Indian-style gardens. Again, best

used as a block overlaid on to a darker colour. It's excellent uplit at night.

Yellow

This colour can be a disaster when used outside – pale yellows just look wishy-washy. Deep yellow can be inspiring mainly when used to colour a structure and on a summer's day it creates its own ray of sunshine. However, it's a tricky colour to be used when not clothed in dark green foliage.

Green

If you want something to disappear, paint it green, the darker the better – use it for concrete walls and ugly sheds. Black is also good for this purpose and

A rendered block water rill is painted red to create a striking highlight against a green garden.

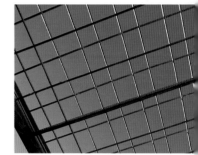

provides a great foil to highlight white-barked trees and richly coloured foliage and flowers.

New materials

The hard landscaping in a garden – which consists of the paved areas, walls and structures such as gazebos and even sheds – has in the past been built from relatively traditional materials. Up until a hundred years ago the major cost factor in terms of materials was transport. Garden features and structures were built from materials available locally, which would often be the same as those used in the construction of the house. This helps to forge a natural link between building and garden and therefore in design terms helps to create a harmonious relationship. It wasn't really until the 1970s that we witnessed a huge explosion in the amount of products that began to be developed specifically for gardens, from paving slabs to multi-coloured gravel. For the first time in suburbia, choice became an issue – the market was developing. People went down to the garden centre, the DIY store or builder's merchant and would pick from whatever material was available.

The results weren't always pleasing, however, and led to a certain uniformity and with gardens not always linked to the architecture of the house. It is only very recently, since architects and artists have begun to explore different mediums and materials, that the possibility of going beyond the norm, when constructing features for the garden, has become an issue. Led by interior fashion, people are now thinking beyond traditional materials and using glass, metal and plastic in new ways. When we look around our homes, offices and workplaces all sorts

of potential materials come to mind. Some of these can be used as new or some as salvaged materials. Metals such as stainless steel and galvanised aluminium have in recent times made their way into the home. But their application in a garden setting is also valid as they are durable and give a new surface for plants to contrast with.

We have long used glass in virtually every other area of our lives, but have been reluctant to adopt it in the garden. This is silly when its transparent qualities are considered and, of course, its horticultural benefits. Many gardens are quite small these days, so using glass dividers can be an efficient and virtually maintenance-free solution. It also offers great qualities when it comes to designing lighting schemes. So materials like metal and glass, when used judiciously, can enhance the link between gardens and contemporary buildings. They can also serve to set a garden in context. This is all very exciting in terms of design, but make sure the materials are suitable for your purpose and, as well as experimenting with new ones, consider whether you could use more traditional materials.

And one last point about choosing materials: newer man-made materials can sometimes have the advantage of being more environmentally friendly. This is becoming an increasingly important consideration as we become more aware of the limited resources of our planet and natural habitats are destroyed because of the plundering of forests and unique stone formations – and even pebbles are removed from beaches

In the next chapter we get back to basics and harness all your new-found inspiration into a coherent garden plan that will suit both you and your plot.

Glass, metal and decking wood are all recent introductions to European gardens. They provide new qualities for design and construction, but also have new obligations for the gardener in terms of maintenance.

BACK TO BASICS

LIGHTING

PLANTING

LAWNS

DECKING

WATER

LIVING SPACE

PLAY AREAS

STORAGE

BUILDINGS

Let's leave the airy-fairy parts of design aside for a while – we will address it later in the case studies, but for now, let's get back to basics. The bottom line is that you want to design a plot that is suitable for what you want but also for the way that you live. This means saying hello and getting to know your garden.

The cleanest starting point will always be to develop a new garden, one with which you have had no previous relationship. The more complicated development results from an existing garden, to which you have a strong attachment, being remoulded to suit a new phase of your life. In this situation it can be hard to go back to basics. However, if your finances and time can't stretch to a completely new garden, it is possible to concentrate on one part of your garden or to renovate and improve the whole plot without any major reconstruction.

This garden possessed a charm of its own, and rather than changing its appeal by pruning or removing trees, cages were built above it to house new living spaces.

OBSERVATION

The first step I recommend is observation. This is going to be the easy part. Have a look at your garden; absorb it. Not instantly – take time to drink it all in. Don't run around the garden like a mad March hare making elaborate plans, just relax. Get to know your garden. Develop a courtship with it. Don't jump into the beds on the first date! You have a magical plot and the possibilities are endless. And don't scream back at me, 'Well, you haven't seen it, how do you know that?' Trust me: any area can be made brilliant. Just remember one thing. You'll never own this garden, you will have custody over it for a period of time. And if you listen to it from an early stage and go with what it tells you, your relationship will be a happy and fulfilling one. If you don't, the relationship will become dysfunctional, the garden centre will become an expensive therapist and the garden will sneer. On a practical level, however, there are a few things that you will have to find out first.

CLIMATE

This might seem very basic, but what's your climate like? Obviously from country to country this changes enormously and the big effect of climate on your garden is to limit or enhance the choice of planting. I grew up in Ireland where the climate is temperate, which means a lack of extremes of either hot or cold, wet or dry. Consequently there was a massive range of plants available to grow. But in your part of the world you might have long, hot summers but very cold winters with lots of frost or snow, so be aware. A local source such as a botanic garden or a garden centre will fill you in.

ASPECT

This means where the sun is at different times of the day – is it a north- or south-facing garden? This too will have a big effect on the type of plants you grow. It is almost like having an individual climate per garden, I suppose, and while there are exceptions to every rule, it will pay off if you place the plant where it wants to be.

The aspect of the garden will not only influence the plants, on a practical level it will tell you where the washing line should go or where the patio should be. When you come home from work at 6 o'clock in the evening on a summer's day, you want your patio to be in the position that makes the most of the last of the sun. This may be at the back of the house, at the end of the garden, or somewhere in between. Or indeed it may be in your front garden.

SOIL TYPE

And now for the science bit. I think the most important investment you will make in your garden is to understand the soil, and the problems or joys that it offers. Getting this right at the very start helps enormously. There are a number of different variations on the basic soil type, which range from heavy clay to light sand.

Ideally you will have what's called loam – a nice, dark, breadcrumb-like structure, teeming with insects and worms. This will mean it has good drainage but can hang on to water and will be fertile. But, unfortunately, you are as likely to have one of the following:

Clay

A bit like Playdough – it is sticky and can be moulded into shapes. It may be full of goodness

The heavily planted background was retained in this garden while a new dramatic garden was designed inside it.

This garden consisted of three raised trays, constructed as though floating at different levels. This enabled us to create our own soil mixture from scratch for each tray.

and nutrients, but the drainage is bad; it gets sticky and flooded in the wet and rock hard in the summer.

Sand

This soil has a lot of sand particles in it and feels gritty – this means that water will drain very quickly from it, which is good, but so too unfortunately will all the nutrients, which is not good. This can be improved by adding organic matter – sand needs frequent irrigation and feeding.

Silt

Half-way between clay and sand, this retains water better than sand and is more fertile, but it tends to get compacted like clay, leading to bad drainage.

Chalk

Pale, shallow and stony. It's quite free draining, which is good as it doesn't get waterlogged, but it will lose nutrients quite quickly. Its pH is always alkaline.

Peat

This is rich in organic matter, dark and moisture-retentive. Great for growing acid-loving plants such as rhododendrons, camellias and heathers.

Don't worry – virtually any soil can be improved with a bit of attention. To improve water retention for sand, silt and chalk soils, dig in plenty of organic matter such as garden compost and well-rotted manure. This will also help to break up heavy soil like clay. Lime can make an acid soil more alkaline and any infertile soil can be helped with fertilisers.

You may have other problems to contend with. If your house is new, the builders will have left you some presents that won't be apparent when you move in. You'll find that every bit of machinery on site has probably used your plot as a roadway and therefore tonnes of metal have compacted what was once maybe virgin land into something approximating the density of hard core under the M25. You might also find that tonnes of rubble have been swept under the carpet, i.e. dumped under your lawn. Maybe the builders have been good enough to give you a sprinkling of nice new topsoil over which they have rolled out a perfect green carpet of turf, but the calm on top may hide some unwanted presents lurking below.

You will also need to find out your soil's pH. This is basically whether your soil is acid/sour, neutral or alkaline. In turn, this will determine the range of plants that will flourish best in your soil. A pH test is very easy to do. Buy a kit, which is comparatively cheap, from your garden centre and follow simple instructions.

So observe everything that's going on in your garden, feel the soil and watch the sun. Now for some good news – don't march out and change everything instantly. We're lucky enough to have different seasons. If you can bear it, let the garden go through all four seasons before implementing your grand plans. Write down what you see. If it's an established garden that is new to you, photograph the changes and paste them into your notebook. Take delight in the secrets that it reveals at different times of the year.

Before you develop your plan, there are two other important considerations – money and neighbours …

A complete garden overhaul, which may even include an outdoor room, will be expensive. But individual features from this garden such as the decks or water rills could be more appropriate to your site and still create a full picture.

BUDGET

You know what you want and what you need. So how can your dreams become reality? It's time to start thinking about money. Creating a beautiful garden doesn't necessarily mean spending a fortune, but it can be an expensive exercise. The first thing to do, which may sound strange, is to totally forget the wish-list you've just made! Don't try to work out what each element will cost and have appropriate estimates done. Instead, decide on what your budget is – you will know how much you have realistically to invest in your garden – over a given period of time. You may be planning on spending only a few interim years in your home or may not have any plans to ever move again. Spending, for example, five thousand pounds might seem frightening, but think of it spread over five years and it doesn't seem so bad. Work out a plan with long-term as well as short-term things you can do to create your dream garden, just as you would do with the inside of your home. Once you have established your overall budget, go back to your wish-list and work out what is possible and what will have to go. When renovating a garden, consider carefully what can be kept. Old existing features in a garden may prove not only useful but economically sensible to retain and could leave you more funds to invest in other areas. Many land-scapers and designers will advise on a clean sweep of a plot, but be wary about removing everything.

Even from day one you can contribute to the overall look of the garden if you use your money wisely. Concentrate on developing your skeleton planting, clothing your boundary walls with choice climbing plants and establishing some specimen trees and shrubs in central areas. I'm not

suggesting you keep a running total of everything you spend, but if you mentally totted up the money you spent on all those impulse buys on weekend trips to the garden centre, you might get a nasty surprise. Just as supermarkets place sweets at the checkout in easy reach of little fingers when they know it will drive already stressed parents to distraction, garden centres put an attractive array of plants right by the tills to tempt you into thinking you want them. But resist. It's easy to fritter away quite a bit of money on an elaborate hanging basket just to give your garden a bit of instant colour or fill your trolley with a few shrubs because you like the look of them at the time. You can waste a fortune putting the wrong plant in the wrong place. (Chapter 8 – Designer Plants gives more guidance on buying plants.)

A secluded cave built into the bottom of the garden allows a place for privacy and late-night entertainment.

NEIGHBOURS AND THE PRESSURES OF MODERN LIVING

The more we live on top of each other, crammed in and jostling for space, the more people tend to barricade themselves in. Man's territorial instincts seem to take over and, when it comes to gardens, disputes over boundaries are sadly becoming more and more commonplace. Most people know of a horror story of a neighbourhood dispute that may have begun as a mere frosty exchange but has escalated into the sending of solicitors' letters or worse.

When you are thinking about your garden design, try to pre-empt what your neighbours might possibly object to. Why not go round and talk to them first? Perhaps they will point out something that you hadn't thought of which will

actually make your garden better in the long run. Above all, be reasonable. They might actually gain pleasure too from looking at your garden out of their windows.

There are other ways of creating privacy within your garden without necessarily erecting barricades – you can excavate downwards, for example. Instead of thinking of fences as keeping people out, think of them in a positive way: they can act as a background for plants or as shelter belts.

On the programme we do take care to talk to the neighbours as well as the owners and we will modify our plans accordingly if they have reasonable objections. Like everyone else, we also have to take into account the many rules and regulations that are in force: some walls are listed, structures over a certain height may require planning permission and different local authorities have different policies. But as far as plans which don't need to meet regulations are concerned, I like to think that most potential neighbourhood disputes can be avoided with a bit of talking over the garden fence,.

DEVELOPING YOUR PLAN

Garden plans are things that frighten people. On so many television programmes you see the designer unroll scrolls of fascinating architectural drawings complete with long lists of Latin names and site specifications. It's enough to make many of us give up there and then and go straight to the Yellow Pages and get a professional in instead. And yet the reality is that drawing a plan is one of the easiest things in the world, and actually when you begin to play around with the possibilities, it's a great deal of fun too.

The lines of this garden were incredibly simple, so we created a formal, symmetrical garden which had at its centre a long, slow-moving canal.

Leaf through any number of colourful plans in garden design books and the secret of garden planning is soon revealed. The initial lines laid out on a garden plan, before the multi-coloured circles representing plants are added, are very, very simple. Gardens are basically developed from straight lines or curves, or a combination of the two. Often the backbone of a garden will be very simple squares or rectangles superimposed on each other.

The great secret to planning a garden that works for you is the thought that goes into the design *before* you put pen to paper. Based on your lists of requirements and desires, make decisions about what's staying and what's going in terms of existing structures, features and plants. The existing features which stay, either by necessity, such as a tree listed by your local authority, or by choice – you may think the tree is just beautiful – will form an

A series of squares and rectangles involving paving, metal walkways and underlit slabs form the basic hard landscaping in this south London garden.

integral part of your new design. Sometimes if you are not sure about some existing planting or structures, it may be a good idea to leave them in until your new garden matures and then remove them if necessary.

Finally, remember to be realistic about what your budget will allow you to do. Less is more when you do it well.

DRAWING YOUR GARDEN

The purpose of drawing the garden is to develop outline plans that free you from all the associations the garden currently has. Hopefully this will help you view the site as a blank space.

To make an outline plan, sketch your boundaries and any fixed features on to a simple sheet of plain paper. What I mean by fixed features are the things that will be definitely staying. Go out with a 30-metre (100-ft) measuring tape, measure your boundaries and sketch them on to a pad. (Use a pencil in case it rains.) Your measurements should be good but don't need to be perfect – unless you are a professional, don't get too wound up about it. Once inside, if you want to, you can draw it more accurately to scale using an architect's scale rule, which gives you the most commonly used scales of 1:50 and 1:100. Photocopy your outline sketch five or six times. Now you are ready to consider your actual design.

The rules of good design

It's good to know about the rules. Now the idea of rules when it comes to designing or planning anything sounds horrible, but bear with me for a moment. Some of them will be common sense and provide you with a lot of freedom rather than restrict you, and others you may discard at your pleasure. Listing the rules may steal some of the passion but believe me that will be reclaimed by the myriad mistakes you are otherwise bound to make!

There are a few standard designs, tricks on which millions of good gardens are based. Don't be afraid of using them. Even if your primary interest is in the planting and you have no enthusiasm for design, use these simple tricks or rules because they will make your planting look so much better.

- In general, you want to lead somebody into the garden.
- In general, you want to make the most of the space available to you.
- In general, you want to create a sense of mystery.
- In general, you want to display your plants in the best way possible.

Whatever style you choose, these generalities will usually be true and here are the best ways to achieve them.

PROPORTION

The main secret of design is to try to work with proportion. A garden has to be balanced and this means that shapes broadly need to have a relationship with each other. The shapes you have put down on the drawing will in turn translate into elements of the garden such as planting areas,

A circular opening in our blue-tiled wall frames views and focal points. It acts as an enticement for the stroller to explore the garden.

achieved. All these individual lines just served to segment the plot, not unify it.

There are no hard-and-fast rules about achieving proportion, symmetry or balance and indeed for most people it's a skill that is inherent but difficult to learn. It's a matter of having a good eye and being able to trust one's own judgement. However, many quirky and fascinating gardens have evolved through throwing these rules to the wind. I am often stopped in my tracks by finding myself viewing a traditional, beautiful garden, which is obviously all wrong according to the rule books but so right in reality. This situation often occurs in front gardens where I will see a plant in a totally inappropriate place, according to the conventional rules of scale and form, but which in fact works because it has been beautifully unplanned. One of the things I love most about gardens is the contrast – one can be very well planned and designed, and next door a big, cloudy, green jungle.

FOCAL POINTS

Focal points in gardens are things that make you stop and look. They can range from statues to lighting effects to water features to specimen trees or shrubs to an open clearing in a densely planted space. They are the punctuation marks of the garden. They can be used to draw attention away from some unsightly feature or they can be used to carry your attention on to the next part of the garden. They make you visually dwell in an area. They are a trick. It may be a beautiful or interesting view beyond the garden that you wish to draw the visitor's attention to – in this case, the view will be your focal point.

lawn areas or paved areas. The size of the shapes must be in proportion to the size of the plot that you are dealing with. Too many small shapes or too many conflicting shapes will create a disjointed site.

In the past, gardens have often developed in this disordered way because they have been unplanned. In a practical sense this means somebody going into their garden on a Saturday morning and creating a bed in which to grow a plant or selection of plants without any thought to the overall unity of the garden. This situation came about when we didn't understand design in relation to gardens. Because of our ignorance it was easier to develop borders in straight lines running down parallel sides of a garden and indeed a concrete path running down the middle, maybe following the washing line or leading to a shed. No balance was

Every visit into the garden is a story and we like a nice beginning, middle and end. Our minds are constantly on a journey, constantly creating a story. Generally, you want to lead people through a garden and so develop a design around a real or visual pathway that leads to the end of the journey, which could be a summerhouse that's never used but just looking at it says restfulness in your mind. It may be a folly that represents history or dreams. But the focal point is a reward, an entertaining reward that creates final fulfilment. If we don't get that, it leaves us feeling unsettled.

CURVES

The simplest way to create excitement using line is to use a curved line because in this way you informally create a visual pathway through the garden. The real magic comes with the introduction of bulk and form – your plants. By drawing simple curved lines on your plan you are actually drawing on the ground. But remember to use simple, curved lines with broad strokes and not prissy scallops. It may be scary at first because one side of this broad stroke is going to turn into what we know as a bed or border and it can seem like a lot of space to plant up, but big blocks of planting look much more impressive and are easier to maintain than lots of smaller beds or borders. Of course, at the end of that lovely curved sweep you want a final focal point – perhaps you want a surprise or a place of rest. But these are only details; decide what they will be later – you can go back to your lists for this. All of a sudden everything will appear so easy.

Curved lines, whether full circles, a simple 'C' curve or a more complicated 'S' shape, may form some excellent base lines around which to build up a garden. In reality, of course, these lines will probably translate as lawns and patios.

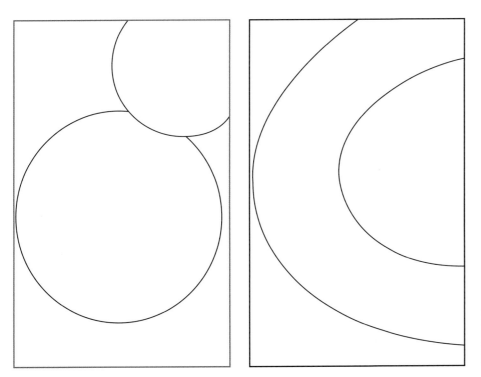
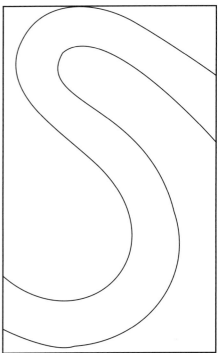

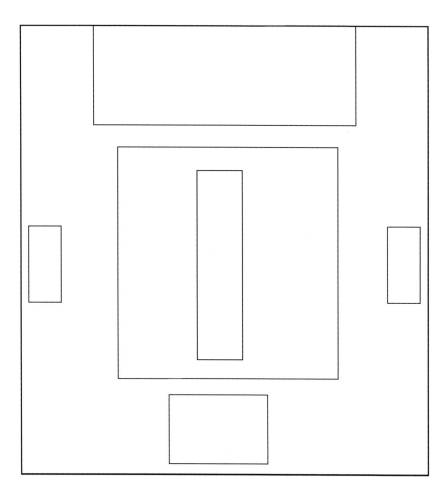

This formal garden plan is made up of a series of rectangles. The central long rectangle could be a canal set into lawn or paving. A patio could be at the top, with a gazebo at the bottom and perhaps two viewing seats on either side. The magic and form will arrive with the plants.

STRAIGHT LINES

Straight lines in the garden often come along with the preconceived notion that they must mean formality. Indeed they can allude to beautifully ordered formal gardens, but they don't have to. They can just mean clean informality, and if you're still not convinced of your artistic flow, this could be an easy way out for you. Many successful gardens are laid out very simply by means of interlocking squares and rectangles. It's a simple device. Recently many of the more modernist gardens have used straight lines, I think generally as a reaction to the softness of rock gardens, cottage gardens and Japanese gardens – all in vogue in the seventies, eighties and nineties. Action and reaction is how styles and trends can develop. Of course, straight lines don't have to run straight out from the house to a determined point. They can also run across the plot and so create movement and some of the intrigue of the curve or S-shape.

TIPS ON CREATING DESIGNS FOR AWKWARD-SHAPED GARDENS

Long, thin garden

This can be an uncomfortable shape to start off with but is a surprisingly common garden shape. The easiest way to deal with this sort of situation is to break up the length into a series of smaller spaces, a succession of garden rooms. This can be done by creating barriers using plants, trellis or walls made of brick, glass or steel (see Dividing Lines, pages 68–79, for more ideas on this). The design solution may be an oft-used one, but the obvious can sometimes be, well, the obvious.

Very sloping, steep site

Different levels in a garden can be fantastic. Straightaway you create real interest. But it can get mad and be maddening. Many gardens are unusable and are such a bore to maintain because of their inaccessibility – try mowing up a hill. They can also be unsafe for children or older folk and completely inaccessible for anybody with a physical disability. The answer here is to create a series of wide terraces with four or five steps or gentle ramps linking them. One terrace could be almost all paving or decking for a garden to sit out in – almost a roof garden or balcony – and then you could look down on your lawn or planted areas. Dramatic use can be made of water in this situation because, of course, you have a natural fall.

Very small garden

Right, in this situation, let's not pretend. You've a small plot, maybe a courtyard garden. You're not going to create the illusion that it goes on forever so don't even try. Lay out a carpet in the centre as you would do in a room – this could be a square or a circle of grass – and adorn the surroundings with plants. Accept what you have, clothe the walls with climbers. Reduce your aspirations, whether they are functional or aesthetic, and treat it as a real room. In this plot plants should be king. Don't be scared of using large specimens here, but don't be stupid about it either. A massive gunnera can look excellent in a small space, but planting an oak tree would just be silly. Don't try to use too many materials in a small area. If your garden walls are made of brick, create the paved area of the same or similar coloured brick. Deal with this plot – don't pretend.

Oddly shaped gardens

Gardens that are triangular or just weird-shaped aren't awkward at all. Who cares about where the boundaries are going or if your plot has been squeezed into a misfit site? The new lines that you create will determine your real shapes. So start off by drawing a large circle and you'll see what I mean immediately – no longer will your eye be drawn towards a corner. Plant the corner. Plants don't care.

Broad gardens

A plot that has more breadth than length can be an unfortunate site. You have the land but it's not usable from the house as you would want it to be. This just means that your view of the garden is

These two line drawings immediately create interest in a garden by leading the eye through the plot. Both are simple, but effective.

This garden was totally based around free-form swirly lines and became the ultimate in playing with curves on both a two- and three-dimensional level. To build it was very difficult. To maintain it takes some dedication but aesthetically, to the owners and visitors, it's intensely stimulating.

probably the shortest view. You have to be quite clever here and determine the design by making sure that when you look out of the window your attention is being drawn sideways. This may be achieved by a large oval shape, the belly of which is your narrow view. Think of a torpedo shape. Maybe have the sound of water somewhere to the left or right of the house, which should draw you out to explore or just give you the feeling that there's more. An informal stepping stone pathway set into the lawn, from left to right, or planting will have the same effect. All these features act as arrows, leading you or your eye across the garden.

TIME TO START DRAWING

Now start drawing. Concentrate on your ground plans, on your main lines. Enjoy the freedom of setting pen to paper, and with a few instruments – a ruler, compass, flexi-curve and, most importantly, an eraser – start to develop your plans.

Remember by now you've done the intellectual bit – you've carefully considered your style and your content. You know it is line and shape that you are after. Anyone can draw. As children we're not scared of attacking a blank piece of paper, but as adults many consider it childish. But it's just an idea that you want to capture, so scribble away, either free-hand, or with a ruler and flexi-curve. You've made several photocopies of your outline plans, so if you don't like what you're doing, throw the sheet in the bin and start again. As soon as you have a plan that you feel works for your garden – and for you – you can begin to translate some of your lines and curves into reality. The next chapter looks at dividing lines – the walls and screens that define your garden.

DIVIDING LINES

LIGHTING

PLANTING

LAWNS

DECKING

WATER

LIVING SPACE

PLAY AREAS

STORAGE

BUILDINGS

Communal gardens demand separate areas, some of which must be places that many people can gather and use. But for your dividing walls, consider new and unusual materials such as glass brick, metal or wire mesh, rather than just reverting to trellis, brick walls or hedges.

Dividing lines mean in effect creating walls and screens in the garden. Be aware of them, but don't become obsessed by them. They may encase your whole garden, in which case you will want to consider creating focal points within the boundaries. Or you might be lucky enough to have a view beyond the garden, be it of a wonderful seascape, towering hills or a pretty village church spire. Whatever the case, boundaries delineate your property. So keep in mind their potential for both trouble and delight.

Walls need not be a visual barrier: they can be see-through, they can frame a view or they can become the actual focal point in themselves. In the garden, internal dividers can be a fantastic way of compartmentalising the space – they are a way of creating a series of garden rooms. Another important reason for incorporating walls in a garden is to provide shelter for plants or to act as a support for climbing plants. This has been traditionally achieved by walls of brick, stone, hedging or trellis, but there's loads of scope for using your imagination and having some fun.

Most of us now live in built-up areas, whether in cities, towns or suburbia, and we constantly strive for privacy. But remember that the effect you want is not to exclude everything, including sunlight, from your garden, so try to create a balance. This is one of the areas where work in your garden will have an effect on your neighbours, so, if you are constructing a wall, work in consultation with them. It also has planning considerations which are individual to local councils and town planners, but generally a boundary wall cannot be higher than 2.2 metres. Walls or screens can be very useful in terms of hiding unsightly structures, such as an ugly oil tank or compost bins. However, the danger is that if they are designed or built badly, they can actually draw attention to what you are trying to hide.

The gardens that we do on *Home Front in the Garden* tend to be very structural. So walls are constructed for their own beauty using a range of unusual materials rather than having a solely practical use. This is something that has been shied away from in garden design. But the link between gardens and architecture is more important than ever before because many of us live in relatively bland houses in suburbia, and structures in the garden can give you a chance to show your individuality.

Walls and screens can also be used in conjunction with planting, for example in raised areas or as settings for seats or water features. And as well as providing a basic structure they offer endless possibilities for you to use paint and other decorative effects.

Walls are such an important part of a garden that they should be a major consideration in your overall design. But there are some issues you need to consider. When you are choosing the style of your garden, decisions have to be made even before you choose your plants, so be aware that thinking about your garden walls *is* important for many reasons.

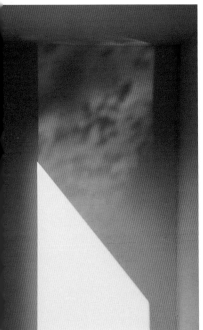

Sheets of steel were used to create tunnels beyond which various gardens were found. In a relatively small space a vegetable garden, water garden and a deck garden could be treated individually.

CHOICES

What are your requirements and what determines your requirements?

- Aesthetics: What will look good and what do you like?
- Local materials: There are some unique characteristics to walling in different localities around the country. Encourage the survival of local crafts and customs and help to create a unique statement by following on with these traditions – if, of course, they are appropriate for your design. An example could be flint walls in Suffolk, while in Connemara dry stone walls are a must.
- Architecture: Think about the buildings nearby and the material(s) used.
- Function: What do you want your wall to do? Sometimes you may want it to be a screen for reasons of privacy, whereas at other times you may need a barrier against the natural elements. For example, if your garden overlooks the sea, you will want a real barrier to stop strong, over-enthusiastic waves invading and drenching your soil with salt, so here a wall of toughened glass could be appropriate.
- Permeability: If you are trying to create shelter from wind, a semi-permeable material is best – a solid brick wall can create more wind problems than it solves, as solid barriers deflect wind upwards, which creates a vacuum beneath them which in turn draws air downwards – in other words, you end up with an even windier site.
- Height: There are planning regulations to consider. It is always best to find out from your local authority what these are in your area as they vary in different parts of the country and indeed from country to country.
- Site and situation: Is your garden very dark and gloomy or open and sunny? This will determine what plants you can grow if you are planning a hedge or planting climbers or wall shrubs.
- Cost: Need I say more?
- Durability: Do you want something that will last a lifetime or are you thinking more short-term?
- Adaptability: Some materials you just have to use as they are, while others you can stain and paint.
- Maintenance: Some materials require more up-keep than others. Are you prepared to put in the time and money?
- Renovation: Do you want to consider renovating an existing wall or would it be better to knock it down and start all over again – perhaps with a different material?
- Security: To my mind security is best achieved through using prickly hedges such as *crataegus* (hawthorn) or *pyracantha* (firethorn). Glass shards cemented into the tops of walls are extremely dangerous and could leave you liable in the event of injury. Barbed wire can give you the feeling that you are living in a prison.

TRADITIONAL GARDEN BOUNDARIES

Here are some of the materials that have been used for centuries to build walls and boundaries.

Brick walls

These are beautiful, warm and pieces of art in themselves because they are hand-crafted. They can be valuable assets for gardeners as they absorb the heat from the sun during the day and release it like a radiator late into the evening. Plants can look great against them. They are, however, expensive because of the high labour costs. Once they go beyond a certain height, the brick may just be a facing on to a background of block. Maintenance can be an issue for old brick walls. If you are restoring a garden, a wall may have to be re-pointed. One big advantage of using brick in a garden is that if the house is also made of brick, the unity between house and garden is immediate.

Wooden panel fencing

This type of fencing is the most common garden boundary material in Britain; mainly because it's cheap, but also because it fits in quite happily in most environments. As the panels will generally not be incredibly sturdy themselves, they need supporting with squared posts. Often they will arrive in their garden in a fresh tan or orange colour which is hideous. If you are impatient and don't want to wait for them to be sun bleached to a nicer, more natural colour, paint them a very dark green. At this stage, they will look beautiful adorned with climbing plants. Two advantages of wooden panels are that the individual panels can be removed for access into the garden if you are having major work done, and also that individual panels can be repaired or replaced as time goes by.

Woven willows

A recent trend has been to create attractive visual barriers using woven willows. Indeed, it has long been common practice in some rural parts of the country, and living or dead willow can be suitable options. However, while looking excellent, it is not very strong. A living willow wall/cage will love a lot of water and will need constant cutting back.

Trellis

Trellis can be an excellent addition in a garden to adorn ugly existing walls, to enhance beautiful brick walls or used with climbing plants to create internal dividing walls. Use only expensive trellis because cheap stuff will not last and this can be devastating if it falls down in heavy winds and takes established climbers with it. To use climbing

An existing uninteresting wall can be livened up with exterior paint and play host to some vibrant, artistic expression.

plants on a framework of trellis set against a wall, hold the trellis a few centimetres out from the wall by means of batons. This will allow good air circulation all around the plants and cut down on the risk of diseases. If installed properly using heavy posts between panels of sturdy trellis, it can make an excellent garden divider because the holes in the trellis allow a lot of wind through and so will not be subject to the same storm battering as a fixed panel.

Hedging

Hedging is the most traditional garden divider of all, forming both traditional and contemporary boundaries because of its boldness of shape. The advantages are clear. You have a beautiful planted backdrop to the rest of the garden, one which can change with the seasons, can be formal or informal and which can grow to whatever height you require. However, most hedging will need a good degree of

maintenance. For formal gardens a yew hedge is king. An evergreen hedge can give great structure to a garden all year around but especially in winter when the skeleton of the garden is exposed. When planting a bed in front of a hedge, take care to leave enough maintenance space in between the plants and the hedge for a step-ladder or platform. Hedging is not an instant-fix solution, so it may be more suitable if you're planning to stay put for a while.

CONTEMPORARY GARDEN BOUNDARIES

Now to move on to some of the most exciting possibilities of recent years.

Glass

Glass is a material that we haven't come to terms with in the garden yet and in our rush to do so we will doubtless make many mistakes. Often people who do not understand what the nature of

Glass bricks make an excellent garden divider as they can separate areas and cut down on exposure to wind. This garden wall is also a water feature with water running down its sides.

While not strictly dividing the garden in the conventional sense, these concrete structures both frame and delineate separate garden areas.

contemporary design is or indeed who do not understand what *design* is will embrace a different material just for the sake of it. A contemporary garden is not one that is constructed just by using contemporary materials. I am sure that as time goes on glass is going to be a case in point. Glass is a dangerous material, one that has to be respected. It is beautiful, but must be properly understood and correctly maintained. It offers possibilities which we haven't seen before, so we will make our mistakes and through them hopefully find good use for this ever-evolving material. Glass is also expensive and this may provide the real reason for our reluctance to use it.

My favourite way of using glass in a garden is in the form of glass bricks. These were very popular world-wide in 1930s' modernist arch-itecture and today, early in the new century, we are very familiar with them. But just a few short years ago in 1996, when I used them to create external walls at a garden for the Chelsea Flower Show, they were an oddity. To construct a wall or boundary using glass bricks, call in an expert. They require the support of steel poles at regular intervals, threading stainless steel bars between every few layers, special mortar and silicone because of different expansion and contraction rates between materials. That's the technical bit.

On the plus side, they offer transparency, different designs, colours, interaction with natural and artificial light, a climbing frame and shelter for plants and excitement for the garden lover. They can be used in conjunction with water to form glistening, sparkling walls. They can be used in curves or straight lines and are as strong individually as clay bricks. Structures made of glass brick can be built very near houses or buildings without dramatically reducing light levels inside them. To my mind, glass bricks are the perfect contemporary garden construction material.

Sheet glass is beginning to come into its own. It must also be constructed by technical experts and in accordance with architectural guidelines. It can be used clear, frosted or engraved. Green-tinted sheet glass is especially effective in gardens and can be used as a backdrop to planting schemes rather than as a host for them. Used in conjunction with fibre optics it carries light. It is extremely easy to maintain but should be cleaned on a regular basis to obtain maximum benefit.

Concrete

We associate concrete walls with raw block walls bonded together with mortar. It's the type of garden wall that I grew up with and indeed the one that my parents still have. Concrete has very bad associations in our minds with inner-city tower blocks and urban decay. It is brutal and uncompromising and so it scares us and we become appalled at the notion that it could ever be used to add structure to the beautiful thing that a garden should be.

But concrete *can* be beautiful. It's a simple material that responds well to various types of treatment. Many wonderful Art Deco houses have been constructed from block, which is then rendered, or poured concrete is used. If you are making a feature of the structure of your garden, concrete can be a good material to use. But plan to give it some character by creating brutal blocks of form in different heights which play off each other for effect and use plant forms as a contrast against them.

Metal brings a sleek and often reflective quality to walls. *Left* Here aluminium plates have been spun into discs and used to tile a wooden workshop wall. *Right* Stainless steel with a satin finish is used to clad retaining walls.

TIPS FOR PAINTING OUTDOOR WALLS

- It may sound obvious, but check that the paint or stain you want to use is suitable for outdoor use.
- If it's paint, it should be masonry paint.
- Do a patch test on the wall first – just as you would do indoors.
- Look at the colour at different times of the day to see how light affects it.
- Prepare your walls well – brush down stone or concrete first with a stiff wire brush.
- Hiring a spray gun from a DIY shop or builder's merchant can be a wonderful time saver.
- If you are spraying walls or fences, make sure you do it on a still day when drifts of paint will not carry into your neighbour's garden and paint their lawn blue.
- Panel fences are best painted with a few thin coats. Apply very sparingly so that drips don't go down the neighbour's side of the fence.
- When painting trellis, try to take it down first if possible. Lay it on sheets of plastic outside. If it is already inhabited, it will be a battle of wits between you and the plant.
- It's rarely a good idea to paint a single piece of trellis a dramatic colour and then put it up against a grey wall. It will end up looking like a cheap Spanish café.

Concrete can be painted and a current fashion is for it to be painted white in a minimal style. But it can also be made more user-friendly by contrasting sections of wall with different blocks of colour. To make an ugly concrete wall disappear, again paint it a very dark green or black and use loads of plants against it. Likewise, a pebble-dashed wall in a garden is rarely a thing of beauty. To remove the offending dash, render it with many coats of cement and paint.

Poured or block concrete will also act as the perfect host to a variety of claddings. One of the most vibrant of these is ceramic tiling. This creates a very stylised effect, reminiscent of either the exuberance of Gaudi's Barcelona or the subdued elegance of the dark blue tiles of the London Underground. Concrete walls can also be clad with shells from the sea or even pebbles.

Metal

Steel, copper and titanium (if you can afford it) can make excellent materials from which to construct or to clad boundaries in gardens. Many of these metals will have a very interesting relationship with planting – some will form raw backdrops and others will be extremely elegant. Steel comes in many forms. The most hard-wearing but most expensive is stainless steel, which can be commissioned in panels or as structures from specialist engineers. The finishes it comes in range from satin to mirror. Mild steel is a raw product which, depending on one's taste, can look stunning or ugly. My favourite way of using it in a garden is to create broad walls of thick steel, which are left to rust naturally. Galvanised steel is often used because it is cheaper and more easily managed than most

options, but it does not wear as well. The shiny surface that it has initially dulls down after time.

Copper is another material that looks beautiful and shiny when used initially in the outdoors. Fairly soon it dulls, but then transforms after a period into a wondrous green.

Titanium, as used on the exterior walls of the Guggenheim Museum in Bilbao, is a material that I am looking forward to using because of its amazing reflective qualities. But it is very, very expensive.

An oval mesh tunnel gives the feeling of time travelling as you progress through a heavily planted bog garden. Sunshine during the day and coloured lights at night enhance the science fiction effect.

OUTDOOR FLOORING

LIGHTING

PLANTING

LAWNS

DECKING

WATER

LIVING SPACE

PLAY AREAS

STORAGE

BUILDINGS

Paving slabs and turf provide hints of what materials will feature predominantly in this dramatic three-dimensional garden.

The type of flooring you choose in your garden will have an enormous effect on the overall feel and use of the space. Many of the criteria that influence your choices inside the house will come into play when choosing outdoor flooring – which materials you particularly like, especially under bare feet, which colours you prefer and your requirements for the area. There's a wide range of materials available which provide great scope for indulging your fantasies and using your imagination.

Often it is good to think about flooring at the earliest stage of garden planning because you have to consider access to the garden and how you're going to get the materials in. Flooring work often involves excavation and the use of hardcore, sand and cement, so access may be a limiting factor. There are other options when access is restricted – a patio can be reconditioned and given a new lease of life by adding new materials, colours or textures.

Be careful when choosing new materials: while some will be perfect for your requirements, others have a limited life span. The most important thing with any flooring is to do it well. It's not something you'll get away with doing badly: it will always show.

A solid foundation for any hard structure is essential. This is particularly important for a paved area to ensure a safe, level surface. Hard core should be well compacted. The damp-proof course is the protection an architect and builder give a house to stop moisture rising from the ground up through external walls. If you heap soil or any material above the level of the damp-proof course on the external wall of a house, this will cause problems. Drainage is also important when paving any area, especially one that is near a building. Always allow for a fall of the finished surface to a land drain.

CHOICES

What are your requirements and what determines your requirements?

- Aesthetics: what will look good and what do you like?
- Architecture: take the architecture of the building into consideration if the area to be floored is attached to a building.
- Site and situation: is it very dark and gloomy or open and sunny?
- Cost: this is a major factor in terms of any hard landscaping material.
- Association: look at the existing flooring in your house – are you going to continue a theme from a kitchen, living room or conservatory out into the garden?
- Durability: any material that is going to be laid outside must be long-lasting.
- Adaptability: some materials you just have to use as they are, while others you can stain and paint.
- Maintenance: consider the implications of the ease – and cost – of maintaining your chosen material.

RECONDITIONING AN EXISTING AREA

It might be possible to recondition a paved area by removing some slabs and replacing them with cobbles or pebble schemes, mosaic schemes or indeed soften with plants. Breaking up an expanse of mature paving can be very rewarding and can often be the solution to brightening up drab patios. To my mind there's nothing wrong with grey slabs and indeed they sometimes mature well with age.

We should never think that we have to rip out everything and start again just because we are re-evaluating an area or have inherited a new site.

WHAT MATERIALS ARE AVAILABLE?

There is a myriad of choice here. From the more traditional turf and decking to such contemporary materials as rubber, glass and metal, choose the surface that best fits your plans and pocket.

Turf

To describe turf or lawn as a garden flooring may seem odd, but that's exactly what it is. We use lawn often in conjunction with other materials to create what is generally a level surface to walk on or as a foil against which to set other materials and plants. You might think that design has gone mad if common grass is to be reduced cynically to an animate modern material. But let's not get carried away. The lawn does a job for us. Without a doubt, the best lawns in the world are grown in Britain. This is because of tradition and climate and it is my favourite groundcover/garden flooring. Rarely do I design or build a garden without it taking centre space and with the development of instant rollout turf my life, and indeed gardening, has become a whole lot easier. Of course, if you have the time and patience, seed will certainly do as good a job and will be lighter on your pocket.

While turf will be among the cheapest options as a surface material in the short term, in the long term it is among the most expensive because of the ongoing maintenance duties of mowing, feeding, scarifying and aerating. But take pride in your lawn as it is often the main draw into the garden. Many

Warm-coloured cobble stones and soft wood make friendly materials to walk on.

Make sure your site is suitable. The best-quality turf will not flourish in the wrong position, such as a very shady corner. Moss will soon invade and dominate as it does like dark places.

Prepare your soil well before rolling out the turf. Time invested in removing stones, weeds and other debris and creating a smooth, level surface will be rewarded by a healthy lawn.

For a good lawn you'll need at least 20cm (8in) of good-quality topsoil and adequate drainage.

If you are putting down a circular or S-shaped lawn, do not attempt to make the shape by manipulating the rolls of turf into these shapes. Lay out the lawn in rectangular or square shapes and then cut out the shape you desire. Don't use a spade to cut out shapes as a spade is ever so slightly curved and will not give you clean edges. The implement you want is called a half-moon.

Laying out a garden hose on the ground is a flexible way of experimenting with different curvy shapes and will provide you with a guide when you are cutting out the shapes.

Finally water, water and more water. Nothing will help to establish your new lawn as well as a good soak.

Lawns don't have to be in traditional shapes. This one was shaped like a fish and also included some running water, carried in a sunken steel RSJ, which provided a refreshing glint.

a business or personal problem has been solved by whiling away an hour behind a mower. Walking behind the machine up and down the garden gives you breathing space to consider your plants and makes you feel in control of your domain.

Decking

This natural material feels wonderful under bare feet. It is very adaptable in terms of shape and colour and is a good material for setting buildings into gardens. It is relatively economical compared to other natural materials and can be fantastic for creating dramatic areas from which to view a garden. It is perfect for use on balconies and roof terraces because of its lightweight nature. However, it hasn't been fully road tested in our climate, so with some decking the jury is still out. It is unsuitable for places that are not open and sunny and will require regular maintenance to make sure it remains non-slip and free from algae and mosses. At the moment, unfortunately, decking is suffering from style snobbery because it's ubiquitous, but don't let that put you off.

Old railway sleepers can make good decks. Their sheer bulk offers an amazing beauty. But when you are buying them make sure that they are free of tar and creosote and use them only in bright and sunny positions as they have no built-in grooves to prevent slipping. Their beauty in terms of construction is that once you get them levelled either on RSJ beams or a prepared surface they never move because of their weight. Beware of beams that are not smooth and may splinter under foot. The only machine that will successfully cut these beams is a chainsaw and to use this you need to be properly qualified, so get in a professional.

Natural stone

Natural stone is always a beautiful, luxurious option and would be my favourite choice for any garden of distinction. In Britain there is a wide variety of soft and hard stones, ranging from Portland to granite to Cotswold to York stone – each with different qualities. Natural stone is available either as a newly quarried or a reclaimed material. In its recently quarried form it is shiny and new and often suitable for contemporary work. Reclaimed stone has the appearance of being softer, worn through ageing, and because it is a natural material being reused it is environmentally friendly. The only way to use these materials is to use them well, so have professional stonemasons or bricklayers lay them wherever possible. Be careful not to use dark stone such as slate in a dark or shady place as the colouring in winter can be oppressive (especially when it rains). Stone is an expensive investment but worthwhile as it is so durable.

Brick

Brick paving became popular relatively recently through the Arts and Craft Movement with designers such as Lutyens using it as a paving material in his collaborations with Gertrude Jekyll. Natural clay bricks are beautiful and smell of quality and tradition. However, used as paving they can have a short life because of frost damage. This can be alleviated by keeping some aside to replace as necessary after damage. Brick paving can be an adaptable type of outdoor flooring in that it can be used to create a variety of interesting patterns. Different coloured bricks can also work together to build up elaborate schemes. Again it is a material that brilliantly links a house or building into the garden.

Wooden decking is an excellent material to use in an open, sunny place. It's particularly effective when used with dramatic changes of level.

Slices of the trunk from old tree ferns are used to make an attractive, informal pathway.

Concrete slabs

These are the basic garden paving material. They are cheap and affordable and have a natural honest colour. They are extremely durable and work well in conjunction with planting, but they do need good foundations and are heavy to work with. Aesthetically they are stubborn creatures – they don't suffer paint or adaptation gladly.

Poured concrete

Poured concrete is flexible as its shape can be determined easily. It can be polished and coloured and is durable and cheap. However, often the dyes are terrible because the colours tend to be pale, subdued and inconsistent. A big foundation is needed for this material and the concrete pouring should be executed carefully.

A simple block of paving slabs makes an excellent place to relax at the end of a garden.

Gravel

Gravel is cheap and cheerful. Plants love it as it keeps their bums dry. It's useful as a mulch to hold back weeds and keep the soil damp. As it is a natural material, it fits in with many styles of architecture and does a good job of linking features in the garden. Gravel cuts down on maintenance and is a good choice in driveways as the crunch of intruders' feet can be heard. On the minus side, it is associated with lazy and instant gardening and isn't good for walking on in bare feet or high heels.

Rubber

Rubber is a material that is new to gardens and which some contemporary designers seem to rave about. I remain to be convinced except when it comes to paving a children's play area or playground as it is a practical and safe option. Maybe the reason I'm not sure about it is because it seems very artificial but, knowing me, next year I'll be proclaiming its benefits! A whole range of tiles is available in various colours and textures.

Glass bricks

There's nothing new about using glass brick set in concrete as a paving material. Many pavements outside shops are littered with squares of glass used functionally to allow light into city basements. The danger of using glass on its own as a paving material is that it is slippery, but set into squares or rectangles of concrete it can be magical. The shape of the glass lenses varies from square to circle and the colours range from a deep blue to clear. My favourite way of making strong use of glass paving is to underlight it with fibre optics. Beware that this is a big job, but once done it will last a lifetime.

Bark is a cheap and soft
groundcover material and
excellent as a mulch around
the base of plants.

Mosaic

Trips abroad have inspired the gardener and designer to use dramatic materials. Barcelona in recent years has been a byword for style, design and exuberance and Gaudi's influence on that city has now arrived with us. Mosaic allows colourful displays to be created based around any design you can think of. It brings us back to Roman times but because of today's technology a wider range of colours, textures and materials from clay to glass is available. Laying a large area of mosaic floor can be expensive and time-consuming so, if you are creating a design to your own specifications, keep it simple. It will cut down enormously on the work. Beware too that large areas of mosaic tiling can be slippery. A mosaic floor could be a centrepiece – a startling focal point in your garden – and can be laid on top of a concrete surface over a period of time. It may be the perfect idea for a gardener interested in arts and crafts.

Metal

Metal is a material that we are trying to come to terms with in relation to paving. It has often been used, especially in the form of galvanised grilles for balcony floors in contemporary buildings. Moving it into the garden creates both possibilities and limitations. The possibilities include raising grilles above planting, thereby creating semi-shaded areas underneath for species that flourish in that type of situation, such as some ferns. The limitations include no high heels for women (or men) and the fact that it does not make for a comfortable surface for barefoot walking. It also heats up dramatically in hot sunshine. Consider these limitations before falling victim to a latest trend.

Metal flooring is a wonderful contemporary material to use in relation to plants. It is durable and easily raised on a framework – although it is suitable only in places where you don't wish to walk barefoot or in stilettos!

WATER, WATER

LIGHTING

PLANTING

LAWNS

DECKING

WATER

LIVING SPACE

PLAY AREAS

STORAGE

BUILDINGS

A marble pond with stepped sides was inspired by visions of Cleopatra's bath.

Everyone wants water in their garden. It's the cry of the nation. Years ago it used to be something exceptional, something exciting to come across from time to time. Somebody down the road might have a pond or there might be a mysterious fountain in a park. They were just there – you had no idea how they worked and you didn't want to know. They seemed to be magical. But as the trend for do-it-yourself gardening exploded with the television shows following apace, so demand for water features has grown. Water in the garden, which was once an occasional jewel, is now common. Of course, as soon as anything begins to get popular, it is instantly derided by the critics, most of whom will have the benefit of lovely water features in their own gardens. Like everything else we are talking about in this book, it's available to virtually everyone now – and some people don't like that fact.

Rarely in the home do we have a chance to admire water as a permanent feature. We turn on taps for a limited period as they are functional objects. We run a bath or have a shower and feel water. We clean with it but we never let it lie because for most of us it would be just impractical to give over any space. Occasionally we have aquariums but here the magic of water is lost as it is captured behind thickened glass and used solely as a base for life forms. Indeed, water in the home is often regarded as a dangerous, destructive force to be contained and managed. We like to be dry and we like our possessions to be protected. But in the garden we're not scared of it and are beginning to celebrate it.

There's nothing new about water being used in garden. It has been one of the essential ingredients of garden design since time began. Yes, it would have started off doing a job, its function being irrigation, and in very hot climates it was used to cool down the atmosphere. Water became a central focal point in eastern and Mediterranean courtyard gardens. Ornate fountains became prized possessions and the combination of water and sculpture sometimes led to drama and humour. Hundreds of years ago you could have been walking through a blissful Italian garden on a sunny day and your chosen path would lead you into a dark, shady grotto. Stepping on an unseen stone would trigger a jet of water to fly from a wall and hit your face. Startled, you would look around and laughing back at you would be a mischievous gargoyle.

So the way water has been used in gardens over the centuries has changed and it is one of those features of garden design that has kept up with the engineering and technology of its day. Throughout history, to control water demonstrated one's power and so it was, and still remains, the ultimate status symbol, gracing grand estates.

The grand estates of today are more likely to belong to multi-national companies than to wealthy individuals, laid out for the entertainment of the masses in the name of profit, but the power of water is no less realised. For many years the Disney corporation has utilised magical water features in its theme parks – lines of water can be shot out from jets, which then appear to bounce around at their own will. Recently this feature has been copied in a more genteel way in exhibition gardens at the Chelsea Flower Show. British theme parks such as Alton Towers and Thorpe Park generate much excitement through their water rides and Las Vegas just wouldn't be the same without its recreation of Venice, including canals and golden gondolas. In fact, and I don't know if I should admit this, crass as it might appear, but for me one highlight of a trip to Las Vegas was fountains dancing in perfect synchronicity to a rendition of 'Singing in the Rain'. Thousands of people stared in awe at this king of water features and water entertainment. But maybe technology has become absurd when we have created the ability to harness the energy from a great natural water feature such as Niagara Falls so that its flow can now be turned on and off at the flick of a switch, or so that it can be desecrated by multi-coloured Christmas lights for our entertainment.

A simple, circular stainless steel lily pond creates an understated reflecting pool at the heart of a formal garden.

THE JOYS OF WATER IN THE GARDEN

So enough of other people's fantasies; what effects can we hope to achieve with the magic of water? Every garden can contain water even if you have only a small patio garden or balcony. It can entertain, soothe, excite, exhilarate and relax. It can sparkle, it can dance, but it can also reflect. It can be a focus or a subtle gift. Here are some specific ideas for you to consider.

Habitat for plants, fish and insects

The range of plants available for us to grow would be much, much smaller without the benefit of ponds. Anyone who has ever visited Monet's garden at Giverny will have marvelled at the water lilies and irises. Having fish in your ponds also adds a whole new dimension to a garden. Wildlife ponds, by being home to frogs, toads and newts, encourage children to care for their environment.

Entertainment

Through contemporary features such as dancing jets in Parc André Citroën or misting machines in modern Japanese gardens, water can provide stunning visual effects. Even the simple task of watering the lawn with a hose can be made more exciting by attaching one of the many commercial toys available. The power of the water can make a plastic helicopter whizz around as the task is being performed, while, on a more elaborate scale, copper pipes have recently been fashioned into ornate sculptural sprinklers.

Creating a link with the natural landscape

Some gardens are lucky enough to be bordered by natural water features – rivers, seas or lakes. Wonderful effects can be had by creating large ponds or even canals in your property, which appear to link up to water on the horizon beyond. Even the sound of running water from a smaller water feature can create that link in the mind.

Creating a new pleasant sound to distract from background noise pollution

The sound of traffic is the contemporary villain of peace in the garden. To counteract a distant hum or a main-street rumble, flowing water can be used to focus attention within your garden.

Creating new focal points

Water used in various forms can create effective focal points. As you travel through a garden and come across a water feature, whether it is a peeing statue, a hideous overturned urn or a snaking rill, you are captivated. In a small garden water is often used as the main central focal point.

MAKING CHOICES

It is not difficult to install a water feature in your garden, but a good deal of thought should be put in before you decide on your final choice. Creating a water feature in your garden means designing a new feature, a fluid feature. Many of the same rules that you have applied to your overall garden design will be reflected here. Straight lines can mean more formal, curved lines can mean more relaxed. Consider the effect that you want to create and choose materials that fit in well with the rest of your garden design.

Many materials can be used to line the main pond area. You can buy pre-formed pond shapes

Large-scale water gardening can enable a flight of fancy. This pond was inspired by a Florida swamp, but was home to many native British species of aquatic plants. The effect of it in this garden was to create a peaceful environment around the studio for the owner to work in.

The pond in this garden was placed immediately outside the back door, enhancing the idea of escapism. An orange-tiled rill kept the water flowing and created a dramatic sound.

made from synthetic materials such as fibreglass. You can build ponds by pouring wet concrete. Or you can excavate, build brick walls, lay a reinforced, poured concrete floor and then tile all the surface areas to make the pond waterproof. Contemporary materials in garden settings can make technically excellent and visually striking ponds. These include glass, stainless steel, fibreglass, perspex, RSJs and tiled surfaces. When we stop trying to mimic the effects of water in nature through streams and rivers and lakes, a new sense of its beauty in relation to different materials can be achieved. Water adds something to all these materials – even to wood. It distorts, glosses, creates an illusion – it appears to change the material. Water can make a material that is otherwise impenetrable, all of a sudden come to life and become curvy. All these effects are dependent, of course, on the water being kept fresh and clean.

There are a number of other factors to bear in mind and these are outlined below.

Safety

Consider carefully what you want – it doesn't have to be an enormous investment. Safety is paramount, however, if you have young children or even if young children that aren't yours have access to your water feature. A few centimetres of water can be dangerous for a child in the garden. But there are water features that are safe for children, including any that store their water in inaccessible reservoirs.

Pumps/electricity

A pump can be added to circulate the water, thereby introducing oxygen while creating a

desired effect such as a fountain or gurgle. To create added excitement by making water appear to fall from one source at a greater height down into a pond below, use a strong submersible pump. When using electricity, always get a qualified, certified electrician as water and electricity can really be a fatal mix.

Position

Pick an open sunny position, not somewhere underneath any overhanging trees that will deposit leaves and cut down on any natural light. If you are using a pump that requires wiring up, bear this in mind when siting the pond and think about whether an existing area of patio will have to be dug up to lay down wires to the house.

Base colour of ponds

When creating a pond or pool, think about the base colour: the material that forms your pool will most likely be seen through the water. Most ponds will be made from a type of liner – PVC or butyl rubber – the colours of which are generally dark grey or black. Dark colours create a sense of mystery as it isn't possible to see how deep the water is. But dark colours need not be confined only to these materials. A tiled pool could be made from dark mosaic rather than swimming-pool blue mosaic. Black or purple tiles will create a luxurious, satisfying finish. A few centimetres of water running over orange or red tiles can feel like a celebration. Stainless steel, whether it be mirror, polished or satin finish, can be a clinical but at the same time a brilliantly minimal host for water.

DIFFERENT TYPES OF WATER FEATURES

Still, reflective pool

Water doesn't need to do anything to be magical. It can just be there. It doesn't need to be big to have an effect. A simple dish or bowl of water or a large still pond has the effect of reflecting light into your garden. This can create an air of tranquillity. It works especially well if the base and sides of your pond are a dark colour.

Fountains

Fountains, either wall-mounted such as a lion's head spouting water into a receptacle, or emerging from a pond or as a central feature in a courtyard garden, are beautiful. They become focal points either seen immediately or encouraging people into a mysterious part of a garden by their bewitching sound. On a hot day they have a lovely cooling effect. Part of their beauty is that they can be turned on or off. So the water may disappear completely from view and can be perfectly safe for children.

Mini-ponds

Mini ponds are sometimes created with pre-formed heavy plastic containers but if you buy one with a lid, both parts can be sunk into the ground and used as the reservoir for water features, such as a gurgling fountain, water pouring over old or synthetic millstones or beach cobbles. The water seems to disappear but in effect it is being collected in your sunken container and being continuously recycled. This is just one example of ways in which to use a mini-pond.

The concrete rill which runs the length of this garden only contains 1cm of water when in full flow. The feature has three reservoirs which are all protected by metal grilles. Water falls from one rill to another, and its sheeting effect creates a sense of intrigue.

Canals/snaking rills

A line of slowly moving water in a garden has a lovely calming effect. It has a very strong relationship with surrounding plants, whether overhanging plants through which the water can be glimpsed occasionally or whether it snakes through a perfect lawn. Create clean lines; water projected at any speed down a man-made rill will make its own forms. A curved rill made of sleek materials such as steel or polished concrete may result in V-shaped ripples being created as the water hits either side.

Waterfalls

Falling water can be magical and entrancing. In nature this can take the form of waterfalls. In the garden we don't need to mimic nature. Sleek effects can be created by channelling water over sheer edges. The result is an energised sheet of water dropping like liquid glass from one level to another. Because many contemporary materials such as glass, stainless steel and perspex are flat, water can be channelled and guided in an artificial way but still retain the essence of mystery of a natural waterfall.

The pond here reflects the opening in the cave. A simple submersible pump was put in the water to create the effect of a bubbling bath.

TIPS ON PONDS

- First, if you are considering creating a pond invest in a specialist water gardening manual.
- Decide how big you want your pond to be. A good tip is to plan a bigger pond than you initially intend because after a year or two it's probably what you'll want.
- It is always nice to have one side created in the form of a gentle slope so that wildlife can access your pond easily and birds can use the edge of the water to bathe.
- One or two sides of the pond should if possible be paved in a formal or informal manner because any pond, even a wild pond in a domestic situation needs a viewing platform.
- You may want to create an internal shelf at a depth of about 30cm (12in) for some planting.
- Introducing water to your pond from another established, healthy garden pond will help wildlife establish.because it will be full of bacteria, larvae, etc. Never take water from natural rivers or streams because unfortunately it may be contaminated by industrial pollution.
- In some areas where the clay is extremely heavy, you may be lucky enough not to have to use a liner at all. Simply excavating a hole will allow water to be retained.
- Remember that water features do need regular maintenance. If you do not have plants and are using an artificial feature, do add a small bit of chlorine to the water to keep it clean. After construction most ponds will cloud up and look very unappealing until they have established a balance of planting and wildlife. Chemical preparations are available for an instant fix or you can wait and help the situation by balanced planting.

Misting/fog machines

While we have been very good over the centuries at exploring the potential of water in the garden in conventional ways, there is still much joy to be had in exploring its uses through technology. Misting machines offer an innovative way of using water in the garden both for practical and for entertaining purposes. Powered by electricity, misting machines disperse very fine droplets of cool water, giving the effect of mist or fog. As a special effect, they can enhance the mystery of a garden, or they can be entertaining – surprising and even baffling the unsuspecting visitor. And as a practical function, misting machines are a great help in growing some species such as ferns.

THE FUTURE

We still have a long way to go in terms of appreciating the value of water in the garden. And although a water feature adds so much to a design, we have to respect water as a very valuable resource, which means saving it and not wasting it. As time goes on and our climate changes, perhaps becoming warmer, this conservation of water will become more and more important. We must remember that gardens are a luxury as well as a necessity and there is a good argument for only growing plants in your garden that will thrive without too much extra help from you. We don't have an automatic right to perfectly green lawns and it can be very much against community spirit and maybe even selfish in the extreme to disregard hosepipe bans during times of drought.

Overhanging plants create a sense of mystery and makes you wonder about the source of the water.

AQUATIC PLANTS

Plants provide the real magic when it comes to pools and ponds. A whole new world of aquatic and often exotic plants opens up. Water adds another dimension to plants – still water acts as a looking glass for beauties to gaze at themselves while ripples gently sway shapely specimens. Remember, though, that with water gardening the plants are not just pretty faces: they are needed to do very specific jobs. Some surface leaves such as those provided by water lilies are necessary to discourage algae and to keep fish cool on a hot summer's day. Ideally, about half your pond surface should be covered with plant leaves. Oxygenators are also needed to starve out the algae, keep the water fresh and provide food for fish.

Wait for a few days after you have filled your pond with water before planting to allow time for the chlorine in the water to disperse. Ideally you should plant only during the growing season – from May to September – so that plants can quickly establish themselves. Plant in baskets that can be easily lifted in a few years' time for pond and plant maintenance. Wait a few weeks for a bit of an ecosystem to develop before introducing any fish.

These are a few of the plants I like to use when planting ponds. I have indicated height and spread (H and S) with each plant. The following plants like water, but to varying degrees. Shallow marginals like 7.5–15cm (3–6in) of water, usually around the edge of a pool, while deep marginals flourish in up to 30cm (1ft) of water. Deep-water plants such as waterlilies will thrive in a depth range of 30cm –1m (1–3ft). Bog plants are happy with their feet permanently in the water and then there are those who like to just lie back and float…

Acorus calamus 'Variegatus' (sweet flag)
Deep marginal. Semi-evergreen, perennial, marginal water plant. Sword-like, tangerine-scented, mid-green leaves have cream variegation and are flushed rose-pink in spring. H 75cm (2½ft), S 60cm (2ft). Likes sun.

Umbrella grass in a concealed pond adds drama to surrounding ground planting.

Waterlilies are most at home in still or very slow-running water.

Butomus umbellatus (flowering rush)
Deep marginal. Herbaceous, perennial, rush-like plant with narrow, twisted, mid-green leaves topped with sprays of pink to rose-red flowers in summer. H 1m (3ft), S 45cm (1½ ft). Likes sun.

Caltha palustris (marsh marigold)
Shallow marginal. Herbaceous, perennial, marginal water plant that has rounded, dark green leaves and bears clusters of cup-shaped, bright golden-yellow flowers in spring. Especially good for small ponds. H 60cm (2ft), S 45cm (1½ft). Likes sun.

Nymphaea (waterlily)
Deep water. The undisputed queen of aquatic plants. Not only does it provide beauty in the form of its exotic blooms, but also its leaves help to keep the water clear and fish cool. Huge range of sizes and colours available. Prefers open, sunny site and still water.

Pistia stratiotes (water lettuce)
Floater. Herbaceous, perennial. Hairy, soft green foliage is lettuce-like in arrangement. H and S 10cm (4in). Likes sun. I'm afraid this is a summer-only plant – it is tender and will be wiped out by frost.

Pontederia cordata (pickerel weed)
Deep marginal. Herbaceous, perennial. In late summer, dense spikes of blue flowers emerge between lance-shaped, glossy dark green leaves. Distinctive bold leaf shape adds definition to your poolside. H 75cm (2½ft), S 45cm (1½ft). Likes sun.

Primula denticulata (drumstick primula)
Bog plant. Robust perennial. From early to mid-spring, dense, rounded heads of flat, lilac, purple, white or pink flowers are borne on tops of stout stems. Mid-green leaves are broadly lance-shaped and toothed. H and S 45cm (1½ft). Full sun or partial shade.

Ranunculus aquatilis (water buttercup)
Oxygenator. Annual or usually evergreen perennial. Submerged stems bear dark green leaves with many thread-like segments; floating leaves are kidney shaped to rounded. In summer produces white buttercup flowers. H 1cm (½in), S indefinite. Sun or shade.

Typha latifolia (bulrush)
Deep marginal. Herbaceous perennial with large clumps of mid-green foliage. Produces spikes of beige flowers in later summer, followed by decorative, cylindrical, dark brown seed heads. Is invasive, H to 2.5m (8ft), S 60cm (2ft). Likes sun.

Zantedeschia aethiopica (arum lily)
Deep marginal. Summer-flowering tuberous perennial. Frost tender. White, unusual flower called a spathe makes for an elegant, cool, architectural plant. H 45cm – 1m (1½–3ft), S 30cm–45cm (1–1½ ft). Full sun or partial shade.

There are many other plants that like to dip their toes in the water but don't like to get soaked. Some are my favourites which look particularly well by the water are gunnera, astilbe, cimicifuga, hemerocallis, hosta and iris. You will find out more about these plants in Designer Plants, pages 116–41.

LIFE IN THE GARDEN

LIGHTING

PLANTING

LAWNS

DECKING

WATER

LIVING SPACE

PLAY AREAS

STORAGE

BUILDINGS

Heating, furniture and ornaments all play a big part in the contemporary garden, as the outside room reflects the inside room.

What does living in the garden mean? It means something different for everyone. But oddly it is something that has been incredibly restricted up until recently. For a lot of people, life in the garden revolves around cutting the grass and doing a bit of weeding. For others it means pruning and perhaps growing vegetables and fruit trees. For passionate gardeners it can mean cultivating, propagating, displaying and growing. The garden can become an obsession, a place to retreat to, but for too many people it's not a place to be enjoyed – it's a job. But now we're beginning to change and that change is immediately reflected in the market place. Commercial bodies are always quick off the mark when it comes to trends such as people enjoying their time in the garden and wanting to make that time last longer, whether that time is from day to evening to night or from summer to autumn. Now that people have more money to spend on their gardens, fashion is becoming increasingly important to them and having something new, whether that be in terms of plants or of something inanimate such as an outdoor heater, is much valued and prized. And it's even sweeter if the neighbours don't have it.

The showcase for these trends is again the media: gardening shows, television and radio programmes, or magazines and books. Life in the garden is seen as aspirational. The way you choose to use your garden is something that is entirely personal. Just because somebody wants to use their garden to enjoy a beer in or even to watch a football match on television, doesn't make their choice any less valid than that of the person who wants to potter in the glasshouse or tend their herbaceous border. The garden should reflect the interests of all members of the household – even those who have no interest in gardening. It should be a democratic place for appreciation and enjoyment. And it's not difficult to achieve this. Households are made up of different people; from babies through teenagers to party-loving yuppies to avid gardeners to retired folk who love to potter peacefully. None should have a monopoly on gardens. This monopoly has been until recently controlled by the gardeners, but now outdoor living is for everybody.

LIGHTING

Creating a lighting scheme for your garden has both practical and entertainment value. Outdoor lighting is practical in this security-conscious era because it deters burglars and other unwelcome parties. For many people the only time they have to spend in the garden is after work, in which case good outdoor lighting is essential. It can also be used to illuminate pathways and steps and to highlight where water is.

From an entertainment point of view, lighting can be magical. Gardens look very different from one end of the day to the other – we're used to that. The sun will travel across our garden and we follow its path by using different areas of the garden at different times and situating features such as patios and beds accordingly. At night the addition of lighting can create enchanting effects. Focal points like statues or trees can be floodlit or up-lit. Water or waterfalls can be spot-lit. The garden becomes a mysterious dramatic place which seems to have no boundaries.

Until fairly recently the range of lighting available for outdoor use was extremely limited.

However, as well as spike lights, you can now use solar lights that absorb the sun's energy during the day and have the benefit of no elaborate wiring, as well as lamps which would not look out of place in a contemporary living room. With new technology, fibre optic lighting is beginning to be widely used and the many uses of neon are at last being understood in a garden setting. Some of these types of lighting are not employed as practical solutions to lighting an area but rather as decorative focal points which can shimmer and entertain.

Although lighting is a finishing touch to the garden, it is actually something that should be planned for at the very beginning. You really don't want to have to uproot plants that are just starting to feel at home in order to have electric cable laid. Always get an expert to install anything that involves electricity.

TYPES OF LIGHTING

Neon

This is a lighting effect used for its excitement rather than its luminescence. It immediately creates images in a viewer's head of New York or

Lights set into a lawn allow a hover-mower to travel over them easily and safely.

Miami, and its architectural beauty can be harnessed to provide a sleek sculptural light. Neon lighting is surprisingly inexpensive, but it is not advisable to use it where children or vigorous pets abound.

Fibre optics

These are new and amazing and it sometimes seems that the technological world is controlled by them. In a few short years, we will be astounded by how we have limited their potential up to now. They provide light in an exciting way. They can be used in inaccessible places, in or out of water, and their main light-giving components need virtually no maintenance. But they do pose a problem as we are unsure as to how to make the most of their potential and there is a desire in contemporary garden work to use them for the sake of using them. That said, they are perfect for under-floor patio lighting through glass or for a night-sky stars effect. They do, however, come at a cost and installation needs to be planned at time of structural building so that they are fully integrated.

Solar lights

These suffer in cloudy climates and the inexpensive ones tend not to be very good.

Spike lights

Relatively traditional garden lighting, these are in effect spotlights sealed for garden use on a spike so that they can be easily placed in the soil. They are adjustable on a pivot so that the light can be angled to any particular feature, such as specimen planting or a statue. It is advisable to leave some loose cable above ground so that they can be manoeuvred around a short distance as required.

Flares and candles

These can provide real excitement and drama, at low cost, when used for special occasions in the garden. For variety, look for scented candles and ones that can float on top of ponds.

FURNITURE

White plastic, wrought iron, teak and canvas sun loungers have been, until recently, the only options with which to furnish a garden. White plastic tends to be hideous but cheap and stackable. Wrought iron has many traditional connotations and can look very, very well in some settings even if not being used. Seeing this type of furniture in a garden just leads the mind to think of rest and recreation. The other big advantage is that it doesn't have to be moved under shelter during long periods in the winter. Teak furniture has been the traditional softer option, either for park or garden benches. The Lutyens bench is a complete classic of design but can be quite hard to adapt for all settings because of its traditional associations. Canvas director chairs or deckchairs have made their way from the film set and the beach to the domestic garden and provide cheap, easily stored, bright, relaxing comfort.

But as gardens are beginning to be used more comprehensively, designers who would only have taken account of the inside of the house or the architecture are galvanising themselves to create new choices for our enjoyment. One-off pieces still tend to be big investments, but names like Philippe Starck are now appearing on some inside-outside furniture, so hopefully prices should start to fall as items are mass-produced.

An underlit path made from concrete blocks with blue-glass lenses creates a stunning catwalk effect. However, this can be more entertaining than practical, particularly in wet weather when the surface can become very slippery.

People have always been inventive when it comes to creating seating areas because outdoor furniture doesn't have to be as well finished as furniture for the home. One of my favourite pieces for a garden is four railway sleepers laid simply over a stainless-steel rectangular frame to make an outdoor dining table. As we begin to create more stylised gardens, ones that reflect our growing interest in the recent history of design, furniture with echoes of the fifties, sixties and seventies is beginning to emerge alongside the very architectural and minimal styles of today. But furnishings don't have to mean spending money – simply by dragging large cushions out from the house, throwing a rug or a few sheets over an area of lawn or moving out the family kitchen table and chairs for Sunday lunch, you can transform a bit of the garden into a comfortable outdoor living space.

Holidaymakers travelling back from Mediterranean climates, or even people viewing pirate movies, love the idea of a simple hammock strung between two trees. It's a fantastic and perfect way to spend an afternoon in the garden.

People like to entertain at home and this often involves eating. So when designing a patio area ensure that enough space is given over for a large table, maybe even a permanent one. A good way to judge a decent size for a patio is temporarily to site a table with eight chairs around it and leave enough room for walking around them.

Barbecues come into the realms of furniture. I prefer not to build barbecues into a garden; I'd rather buy portable ones that can be moved around the garden or under protective cover if it rains. A barbecue that is built into a garden always looks lonely and deserted when it's not being used.

TECHNOLOGY

This is a controversial part of garden design and comes back to the debate about what a garden is and what it should be used for. To many people gardens are a retreat from the modern world. They are an escape from telephones, computers, faxes, television, the Internet, music and noise. The last thing that these people want outside is machines that disturb. A garden can be escapism, a man-made refuge created in a preferred style. But it can be other things too. Think of Italian families in a village piazza gathering under the shade of a vine to enjoy life. Now think of your own family gathering on a Sunday evening to project a movie on to a white wall or billowing sheet, seated under outdoor heaters and enjoying a barbecue.

The decision to use the garden in non-traditional ways and explore new possibilities is a personal choice. But as new technological components become available, they should not threaten anyone who doesn't want them. However, as many people in the same household can have different requirements, technology need not be completely ruled out. We have been very slow to embrace technology in gardens because, I believe, of the desire to escape. But also we have not let our imagination work in certain regards. We only allow entertainment through whimsical statues of bare-bottomed beauties, humorous gnomes which fish and illusions with mirrors and *trompe l'oeil*.

All around the world people watch television. Football matches, cricket and horse racing often take place during the hours of daylight and thus result in a retreat from gardens into the home. Saturday morning children's television can only be enjoyed

An outdoor concrete bath has a room created around it. This is the ultimate in luxury and privacy at the end of a mysterious garden.

A practical den for adults and plants alike.

indoors. But now we're in a position where we can use all the modern wonders to turn our patio into a multi-coloured dance floor for that special family occasion, to pipe our favourite music to certain areas of the garden, to create moods and ambience with lights and music, to surf the internet from the tree house and to transform the garden shed into a 21st-century office. All these features can compete with arum lilies and *Crocosmia* 'Lucifer' to be appreciated and to entertain us. Or we can just relax with daisies in the lawn, a beautiful old apple tree and the sound of a babbling brook. Either is attractive and stimulating, but the choice is ours.

When you know you want to install any type of technology outdoors, consider it as part of your overall design from the earliest stage of planning. Just as new office blocks are designed not only to house the current wave of cables and information technology networks but also to take into account space for the infrastructure of what is to come, so you must plan ahead for any installation of garden technology infrastructure. There is nothing more frustrating than having technology in the garden, even something as simple as a water pump or outdoor light, that doesn't work. Spend money on ensuring that your cables and related paraphernalia are laid properly by qualified electricians/engineers so that any problems that may occur can be successfully and easily sourced. Keep a record of exactly where your sealed cables are running under the garden, to what depth they have been laid and where junction boxes, sockets and outlets have been positioned. Have them installed after your initial earthworks have been completed but before hard landscaping such as the laying of paths and patios and making of ponds has been done. Gardening is all about cultivation and you will be a much happier digger if you are armed with this knowledge.

Consideration must be given to the community you live in when installing something different. Noise pollution emitting from inside or outside the house is a modern problem. So if you are planning an outdoor entertainment centre, consider the effects that this will have on your neighbours and how you will manage the process. Some practical considerations should also be borne in mind. If you have a television in the garden, it will be difficult to view in sunny areas, so provide some shade. If you are screening a movie in a garden or beaming slides, you will need a flat white surface on which to show them.

DENS

Children love to escape in a garden. They love places to hide. When I was a child I was fascinated by tree houses and tried unsuccessfully for many years to build the perfect escape in a hawthorn tree. Children want a place to go that is small and enclosed. A tree house is a term, I believe, that doesn't only apply to structures built in trees. A normal garden shed could be adapted to have a secret entrance and compartment at the back that the little ones make their own. If your house lacks peace and quiet, a shed could be converted to a warm dry place in which homework is done or computer games played. But the more secretive the location and the more exciting the journey to that place is, the more special it feels for the occupant. It also encourages positive memories of gardens and journeys through them for later life.

Flash Gordon has landed and left his aluminium spaceship behind, while an enclosed slide gets rid of the need for the children to climb down the levels in a steep garden.

DESIGNER PLANTS

LIGHTING

PLANTING

LAWNS

DECKING

WATER

LIVING SPACE

PLAY AREAS

STORAGE

BUILDINGS

Agave (top) and *Cyperus papyrus* (paper reed).

The term 'designer plants' has been very much in vogue in recent years as the media, and television programmes in particular, have become enamoured with gardening in all its forms. I'm going to use this term in a very loose way to illustrate the ease of designing with plants. You know that old phrase used by pet-rescuers year after year, 'A dog is for life, not just for Christmas'? This could be a good attitude to have about plants. It is unfortunate sometimes that the makeover programmes on television and the exhibition gardens at horticultural shows worldwide cannot possibly, with their time scales, give a realistic version of gardening with plants. In my own field, working on *Home Front in the Garden*, this is the area that is most criticised. However, I think that our job as garden designers on television reflects exactly what has been done in the landscape industry for a long time.

On a personal level, plants remind me of people and different gardening experiences over the years. I have been planting gardens for eighteen years and I am constantly learning. Some things can't be learnt in a lecture hall. It's people and their passions that really inspire and make you think about plants. Watching my boss Josephine Keaveney in Mackeys, an old established seed and plant shop in Dublin city centre, was enlightening. She was very, very strict but she had a twinkle in her eye – and she had a ferocious amount of knowledge and an adamant style. Every day, trays of plants would arrive from the garden centre and would be laid out on the city centre pathway at the front of the shop. Sometimes the display would be so exuberant that the police would tell us to shift some of the plants inside as they were causing such a stir. It was through Josephine that I learnt what a herbaceous plant was, what a shrub was and I sorted out a million bulbs as they came off the container from Holland. Sometimes she would catch me bluffing to customers and put me and them right on the spot.

So a few years later, heading off to college, I was sure I knew it all – what a rude awakening. Peter Hynes had grown up in the grounds of Birr Castle, one of Ireland's greatest gardens. Des Carton had grown up in the city. I would trail behind both during lunch breaks as they admired the cedar on the rockery and the handkerchief tree down by the lake, and I would pick up snippets and be madly jealous of their knowledge.

Years later, with competent planting schemes under my belt, I met the Crocodile Dundee of the gardening world – Neil Pike. He taught me about the *Dicksonia antarctica*, the *Xanthorrhoea* and *Jubaea chilensis* and described with some passion his conviction for the conservation of and education about these amazing exotic species. I was familiar, as everybody was, with the clearing of Amazonian jungles by multi-national companies to make grasslands for cattle, but amazed to hear of similar stories from Australia.

Inspired by these people and many more, I gained some confidence in tackling gardens, getting to know plants and working with them, seeing how they liked each other. Combinations are the key and it's something you never stop learning. It's actually quite hard to write about in a situation like this because it's very personal. Designing planting schemes for *Home Front in the Garden* and buying and laying out the plants is a solitary job. It's always unnerving and generally it's a long time before I know if I got it right.

Plants have always been prize possessions, right through the history of civilization. The Dutch tulip craze of the seventeenth century is an extreme example of how sometimes the price of a single bulb could be equal to that of a house. Obviously this is absurd, but it illustrates how the words 'trendy' and 'designer' didn't just appear in our horticultural vocabulary in the 1990s. It is fantastic having a passion for plants and whether they are the new arrivals to a saturated market or to pages of glossy magazines doesn't matter. So in this chapter I explore recently popular, or designer, plants, other plants and, of course, old favourites. I think the important lesson is to keep an open mind. Let's not bicker but share in the enthusiasm of planning, searching, purchasing, planting and growing plants.

In pre-Victorian times, the range of plants was fairly limited. The Victorian era was the age of the plant-hunters – keen plantsmen who travelled the globe in search of exotic plants to bring back to their patrons. Today you don't have to travel far as garden centres have self-seeded all over the country. But it can be difficult to choose from the bewildering variety available and very easy to spend a fortune on plants that will not ultimately suit your site or taste. So here's my guide to modern-day plant hunting.

Old favourites like the *Choisya ternata* in the middle of this border provide permanent structure and interest but need to be surrounded with other plants to create a dramatic effect.

THE GREAT PLANT SEARCH

Gardeners are a generous lot, be it with advice, plant material or praise. Gardening need not be an expensive hobby. Many a glorious garden has been built on the generosity of others and gardeners are scavengers by nature. Years ago I can remember listening to a great Irish gardening lady, Madeleine Jay of Mount Usher Gardens, bemoaning the visitors who arrived with secateurs in their hand-bags and shopping bags at her glorious paradise in County Wicklow, Ireland. This was on a primetime radio news programme. People who seem to be otherwise upstanding pillars of society develop into passionate garden thieves in a Fagin-like pursuit of their horticultural dreams. It always seemed to me to be amusing, but I'm sure it is infuriating for diligent garden owners. So let's look at the socially acceptable ways of getting hold of the plants that you would like to see in your garden. First, though, you must decide which plants are your favourites.

BACK TO THE NOTEBOOK

By now your notebook should be full of all sorts of dreams and aspirations but hopefully it has plenty of room left for the garden's main components – plants. Many of your desires may have originated from memories of past gardens – what your mum and dad used to grow out the back or in the allotment, or even what you saw growing in a local park. What we call old-fashioned today were the fashionable plants of their day: roses, sweet peas, lilacs. Others will have originated from different experiences, such as watching sci-fi programmes on telly and marvelling at the scary vegetation on planets visited by Doctor Who in the Tardis.

By looking through your notes you will see certain likes and dislikes beginning to emerge. Do you like evergreens such as conifers? Or do you prefer to see the seasons marked by leaves turning golden and falling to the ground? Generally a balance in favour of deciduous – those that lose their leaves – seems to work best visually. Do you like lots and lots of flowers or do you prefer stark, clean, architectural plants? What colours do you like? Is fragrance important to you? Do you want to grow herbs? Choosing plants is as personal as choosing the clothes you wear – forget about

Xanthorrhoea australis
(grass tree).

fashion, choose what you like and what suits you. Buy a good reference book and check out if your likes are suitable for your plot in terms of soil preferences and sun versus shade (see Chapter 3, Back to Basics).

CREATING YOUR PLANTING PLAN

There is a logical route to follow when planting a garden for the first time and once you have your passions firmly in your notebook, begin to get practical and see what you need to start off with. You should have arrived at the stage where you know your garden and soil type and have constructed most of your features. Your central ground-cover area, quite often the lawn, has been laid and your garden is now one big confusing container complete with its own micro-climate of sun traps, shady areas and wind tunnels awaiting its plants. So where to start?

Well, don't tackle everything at once. Even if you have lots of pots and plastic bags full of refugees from your last plot which are now sitting on the patio, delay introducing them to their final resting place for a while. Instead, create your planting plan and use it as your guide when you go shopping.

Everybody has a different way of creating their planting plan and many people have their own rules. Planting plans for the novice are best developed over time. To really learn about plants you need to grow them and observe their ways and eccentricities. There is very little point in setting rigid schemes down on paper during your apprenticeship as a gardener. Once you have caught the bug, knowledge and information will come thick and fast. The solid rules that have developed over decades tend, on paper, to demystify the art, but adhered to stringently they can also remove some of the joy. Personally, as a working gardener, I commit my plans for structure to paper. Once out of the way, my planting plans develop in my head and they are often influenced by regular visits to nurseries. Whether you are planting for a client, and so following close guidelines, or planting your own garden, you always have room to express yourself.

Contrasting foliage, colour and form is something that is learnt by observation rather than thought. It is slightly complex because people's perceptions of plant groupings are constantly changing. Visits to gardens such as Great Dixter constantly inspire, but so do the new trends which are leaning towards more naturalistic planting – some currently coming from Holland and others from America. Be original. Decide for yourself what you like and what you don't like. It may be you that inspires and exports a new trend.

Colour schemes are subjective. Don't be afraid of conforming and certainly don't be afraid of innovating. People have completely different tastes in clothes, cars and wallpaper, so why not in plants? There are currently about four gangs, members of different schools of thought – the Jekyll devotees, the gravel gardeners, the new wavers of grass and perennial planting, and the Zen-like minimalist planters. Form your own gang or join another. I love all sorts of colours in plants. My real joy is always the contrast of the main colour with green. I love a lush green background, which is almost stately, and then bursts of oranges, reds, blues or greys. I appreciate Gertrude Jekyll's melting of one shade into another, one colour into the next to

The gorgeous flower of
Kniphofia **(red hot poker).**

TIPS WHEN BUYING

- Always check the height and spread of a plant and what soil it is suitable for.
- Don't be tempted to buy something just because it is in flower – it is better if a plant is in bud.
- Buy healthy plants – check for obvious signs of disease. Check roots are not coiled, overcrowded or protruding from the pot. Beware if compost drops away from the plant when it is removed from the pot – the plant may have vine weevil.

form a harmonious composition rather than a raucous riot. I'm fascinated by Vita Sackville-West's all-white planting, but not impassioned by it. A green jungle scene would probably be my garden ideal but that's this year. In my notebooks I'm noticing a worrying trend towards old climbing roses and statuesque conifers. Sometimes I try to fight these things, but my mind keeps returning to that beautiful pink *Rosa* 'Cécile Brünner' with its gorgeous scent.

SHOPPING FOR PLANTS

Now you've decided what you want, you can go shopping. The garden centre is the best outlet for your purchases. This is mainly because many of the people who work in garden centres are trained horticulturists who possess a lot of knowledge. That point-of-sale knowledge about a plant you are buying is invaluable. The Horticultural Trade Association produces a range of leaflets on virtually every subject to do with the garden. These are being continually updated and will inform the novice gardener of the ABC of plant life. So for free verbal and written advice, without doubt the garden centre is the best place to shop. As well as plants, the garden centre offers a full supporting role for all your gardening needs, be they fertiliser, bamboo canes, gift vouchers or often a cup of coffee! A visit to a garden centre is a social and recreational occasion, one that is more and more geared towards every member of the family.

As the parallel form of life called the Internet develops, gardeners (like everybody else) are wondering what effect this new type of communication will have on their world. My

prediction is that gardeners love to see, touch and smell their plants before they buy. They like to pick out the specimens themselves, so for people who love their plants the Internet will be a no-no for shopping, save for the nurseries that deal with rare and exclusive specimens. In this case, the gardener will take the whiff of any leaf and be happy. For others who will build a garden by numbers, the Internet will be the local convenience store without the queues and the car park hassle.

Other avenues to be explored include houses and gardens open to the public which set up a stall by the exit gate, cuttings from friends who want either to share or to boast, and specialist groups/ societies which celebrate the mysteries of one particular genus. All have their place, but some of these will be for the more experienced gardener only.

SHOULD YOU BUY MATURE SPECIMENS?

In Britain we are only just coming to terms with the idea of buying mature specimens – something that has been common practice for a long time in many other parts of the world. But our limit with regard to what we spend on a plant has usually been in the range of £3 to £10. To pay £100 or a couple of hundred pounds for an established plant in a pot was seen as vulgar, cheating and suitable only for new money or golf courses. However, the addition of a small number of bigger plants, whether they be trees, shrubs or herbaceous perennials, can change the appearance of the newly planted garden. I would recommend it, providing that buyers understand their obligation to look after these plants. Generally this will mean quite a

bit of extra water and possibly firm staking until they are established.

The effect these plants have on the new garden is to create a feeling of maturity and, therefore, hope. If you have three such plants, you will feel you have achieved something and the wait for the rest of the garden to mature will not seem so long and can be enjoyed. A mature specimen is a thing of beauty. Somebody else has nurtured a plant for many years which now finds itself a home in your garden. If possible, purchase plants that have been grown in this country or ones that have got used to our climate for a period of time before being sold.

PLANTING

The essence of planting is simple. It centres around soil and getting that right, so good preparation is vital. I prefer to work with situations rather than work against them. Knowing something about the

---

HOW TO PLANT

● Water the plant while it is still in its pot.

● Dig your planting hole roughly three times the size of the plant container.

● Give your chosen plant a bucketful of what it likes in the dug hole. This could be well-rotted manure or good-quality garden soil or compost. If it is manure, make sure that you a have a good layer of soil separating your new plant from its food.

● Tip the plant gently from its pot and examine the roots for vine weevil. If the structure begins to fall apart, it will be very apparent that you have a problem. If you do, dump all the material in a plastic bag and take it back to the garden centre. Otherwise gently tease out some of the roots. This will break the rootball and encourage new roots to advance into the surrounding soil.

● Backfill an amount of soil into the planting hole to bring your newly placed plant to the required level. Replace excavated soil around the rootball, firm down with your hands and water well.

Chamaerops humilis (dwarf fan palm) adds a new and exotic dimension to a fairly traditional border.

soil type that you're dealing with is essential (see page 53). Having some knowledge about your chosen plants is also essential.

Consult your planting plan and then gather your plants together on the lawn. They will form a motley crew. Often it's the first time they'll meet each other, as part of the fun of planting is the hunting around for them. So whether they've arrived from the nursery, the garden centre, the Internet, the village hall sale or a contact in the alpine society, have a look at them as a group and take pride in your dating agency. Set them out in their pots on the newly prepared beds and play about with them.

Plant combinations like this *Hosta* (plantain lily) in the centre, *Phormium tenax* (New Zealand flax) and the yellow flowered *Ligularia stenocephala* reflect personal likes and dislikes as much as horticultural tradition.

Position them as you see fit. Water them to make them heavy and stop them falling over. Plan to plant some of your stalwarts in groups of three. Begin to develop an eye for associations and then plant. Work from the back forwards. Water slowly as you go, allowing time for the plant to have a good drink.

Plants, like us, prefer to be seen from their 'good side'. You will often find that by simply turning a plant around, it will look better. And sometimes plants like grasses are best planted tilted slightly towards you, rather than bolt upright. But that's only instant gratification, because in time the plant is going to grow the way it damn well wants to.

THE DESIGNER PLANT LISTS

It's not the fault of a plant when it is labelled 'designer'. It just reflects the current trends. By using these species on television or in magazines we unfortunately tend to sustain this dubious reputation. However, these are the plants that I am currently infatuated with and some old flames too. Height and spread (H and S) are indicated for each plant but will vary a lot according to your site, soil type, climate, ultimate age that the plant achieves and the amount of love and attention it receives. Information is also given here for each plant on the aspect and soil it prefers, whether it is evergreen or deciduous and when it flowers.

Left Dicksonia antarctica
(Tasmanian tree fern).
Above The shiny, smooth
surface of the blue tiles
offsets the ribbed texture of
the *Hosta* leaves.

CLIMBERS The one job I always think is worthwhile is to establish some boundary planting such as hedges or climbing plants around walls or screens.

These plants need time to establish. In the first year or two they may appear just to sit in the ground casting a savvy-yet-suspicious eye around before they race towards the finish line. Even if the garden is going to be given over to the children for some years as a football field or cricket pitch, get this job done and then retreat to the patio and container gardening.

Your decisions in terms of this type of planting will be all the usual ones. Do you want something evergreen or deciduous, flowering or non-flowering, what colours do you like and what are your site and situation like – sunny or shady, hot or cold, wet or dry? After that, it's down to the individual like or dislike of a plant you choose for that particular site. Sounds complicated, maybe, but when you consider that you might be looking for only ten to fifteen climbing plants at this stage to clothe a garden all year round, it's not so frightening, is it?

LIST OF CLIMBERS

Actinidia kolomikta
A truly exotic climber. This has rewarding leaves that are green, cream and pink. Deciduous, likes sun and well-drained soil. H 4m (12ft).

Ceanothus 'Gloire de Versailles'
This plant really has to be seen to be believed. Masses of powder-blue flowers let you know that summer has arrived. Likes an open sunny position in well-drained soil. It's actually a shrub that can be trained against a wall. Deciduous. H and S 1.5m (5ft).

Chimonanthus praecox (wintersweet)
A shrub best treated as a climber. One to impress your friends with in mid-winter when its delicate, pale yellow, waxy flowers bloom on bare wood. To my mind the sweetest smelling of them all. Place in the sun, preferably in a protected position. Deciduous. H 2.5m (8ft), S 3m (10ft).

Clematis
All clematis need climbing frames such as trellis. *Clematis armandii* is the evergreen clematis and is very useful for covering large areas with lush green leaves and white flowers in spring. This is a plant prone to rampant behaviour and will cost a little bit more than many deciduous clematis or other climbers in the garden centre. Needs a sheltered, sunny site. H 3–5m (10–16ft), S 2–3m (6–10ft).

Clematis 'Jackmanii'
This bears large, star-shaped, velvety, violet-purple flowers. Gorgeous rambling through a white climbing rose. Flowers in mid-summer. H 3m (10ft), S 1m (3ft).

Clematis montana var. rubens
This is a pink-flowering and vigorous clematis, flowering abundantly in late spring. Great quick cover for a drab shed. H 7–12m (23–40ft), S 2–3m (6–10ft).

CLIMBING/RAMBLER ROSES:

It may seem traditional but they can be very useful in toning down the effects of contemporary structures in 21st-century gardens. Heavy feeders. Some of my favourites are *Rosa* 'Madame Grégoire Staechelin' and 'Zéphirine Drouhin' – both pink and scented, 'Climbing Iceberg' – white, tough and flowers prolifically, and 'Gloire de Dijon' – fragrant, creamy-buff-coloured with apricot and yellow tints. Roses generally like sunny, south- and west-facing sites, sheltered but not too sheltered from wind (not enough circulation of air will create susceptibility to fungal infections).

Chimonanthus praecox (wintersweet) has a powerful intoxicating scent.

- By their very nature, many climbing plants will be planted at the base of stone or brick walls. These areas can be very dry. Rather than planting directly at the base of the wall, dig your planting hole about 20cm (8in) out, add a good feed of well-rotted manure, and lead the plant towards the wall with a bamboo cane.

- The exception to the general rules of planting is clematis. Rather than planting at ground level, as with most climbers, trees and shrubs, dig a bigger planting hole and place the clematis stem and rootball up to 12.5cm (5in) below ground level. This will allow the plant to rejuvenate from the base in case of attack by clematis wilt.

- The root and shoot systems of clematis have opposite requirements. The roots like to be in the damp shade and the stem and leaves love to be in an open sunny position. So after planting, water, then place some flat slate around its base.

- Many climbing plants need a support system. Some, on the other hand, have aerial roots that will cling to the exterior surface of a wall, building or fence without any assistance. These include *Hydrangea anomala petiolaris* and ivy. If you are constructing a framework such as trellis for a rambling climber, rather than place it directly on the wall, first attach the trellis to some wooden batons. This has the dual advantage of allowing good air circulation around the plant and so cutting down on disease potential, and also making the removal of the trellis and climber possible so that surface wall maintenance/painting is made easier.

Fremontodendron 'California Glory' (flannel flower)

Shooting star of the climbing plants/wall shrubs. Evergreen. Needs good support. Interesting furry leaves and bright orange flowers bring a smile to your face. Flowers in late spring to mid-autumn. The hairs on the stems and leaves irritate some people's skin, so use gloves when handling. Prefers a sunny, sheltered spot in well-drained soil. Very fast growing. H 6m (20 ft), S 4m (13ft).

The complexity of the flowers of *Passiflora* are a testament to nature's artifice.

Hedera helix (ivy)

Always a useful plant as it is self-clinging and will do well in shady areas. Can be used as a climber or a ground-cover plant. 'Buttercup' is one of my favourite of the ivy family – its rich yellow colour reminds me of Irish butter. Cut back vigorously in the spring. H 4m (13ft), S 2.5m (8ft).

Humulus lupulus 'Aureus' (golden hop)

Herbaceous climber with yellow-green leaves and drooping clusters of flowers in autumn. Needs a climbing-frame-like trellis, which it will cover rapidly. Sun or semi-shade. H to 6m (20ft).

Hydrangea anomala petiolaris (climbing hydrangea)

This is a wonderfully useful plant and will grow well in sun or shade. Self-clinging. Deciduous. Brilliant white flowers. H to 15m (50ft).

Lonicera periclymenum 'Graham Thomas' (honeysuckle)

Deciduous climber with fragrant flowers in summer. Prefers sun and well-drained soil. Beware though: it can go rampant. H to 7m (23ft).

Parthenocissus tricuspidata (Boston ivy)

This is a vigorous, deciduous climber that puts on an impressive display of crimson autumn colour. It grows in the shade and is great for covering uninteresting house walls, without the aid of a climbing frame. H to 20m (67ft).

Passiflora caerulea (passion flower)

An unusually exotic plant that produces dramatic white and blue flowers in summer as well as yellow fruit. Very vigorous evergreen – a heavy feeder. H 10m (30ft).

Solanum crispum 'Glasnevin'

Vigorous, evergreen to semi-evergreen, scrambling climber with clusters of lilac flowers with distinctive yellow centres in the summer. H to 6m (20ft).

Trachelospermum jasminoïdes (star jasmine)

Evergreen climber with very fragrant white flowers in summer. Needs sun, a climbing frame of some description and well-drained soil. H to 9m (30ft).

Wisteria sinensis (Chinese wisteria)

The queen of climbers but only to be considered if you are prepared to wait, as it can take up to seven years to establish itself. When it does, it gallops. The flowers are worth waiting for – long, drooping bunches of fragrant, lilac blooms. Looks wonderful hanging through a pergola. Deciduous. Likes sun and fertile soil. H to 30m (100ft).

TREES

At one stage, most of Europe was covered in trees. Sadly, this is no longer the case, but to my mind, no garden is really complete without at least one tree.

Recently, we have seen the devastating effects of climatic changes partly as a result of the clearing of Amazonian rainforests. We cannot underestimate the job that trees do for us by stopping soil erosion, producing oxygen and creating a habitat for wildlife. In cities and in gardens they cut down on noise pollution and help to screen ugly structures and create privacy. I have no doubt that in the future it will be a necessity for every person to plant trees for the survival of our planet. As gardeners, we often plant them for selfish reasons. Nothing gives me more joy in my job than tearing up concrete or tarmacadam and creating a suitable environment for trees. I think this is one area of the garden where we have real obligations to community, humanity and future generations. So even if you have no passion for the outdoors, it is vital to get involved in some way, be it through a voluntary organisation or writing a letter to your local parks department.

On a purely aesthetic level, the range and choice of trees available for our use is vast. Like climbers, trees can be introduced to your garden at any stage and in these days of containerised plants they can be planted at any time of the year. If you have a vast space available to you, it's almost an obligation to consider using some of our native varieties such as oak and hawthorn. But it is important to choose the right one for your plot: always check the height and the spread and what type of soil it likes (well-drained, dry, acid) as well as the position (shade, semi-shade or sun). The cedar is a majestic tree and reminds me of my days studying in the National Botanic Gardens in Dublin, but it becomes far too large for the average garden. Do not plant trees too near the house as they will block out light, and remember that very little can be grown under a tree in full leaf in summer.

Here are some of my favourite trees that are suitable mainly for small to medium gardens.

Acer griseum (paperbark maple)
This is an excellent specimen tree – it has beautifully delicate, peeling bark in rich shades of chestnut and cinnamon brown. It's deciduous, with its leaves turning orange and red before falling. Prefers sun and well-drained soil. H and S 10m (33ft).

The trunk of *Betula jacquemontii* (Himalayan birch) makes it one of my favourite trees.

Acer palmatum 'Dissectum Atropurpureum' (Japanese maple)
Great for creating an oriental feel for those interested in the Japanese look and great when space is at a premium as it is generally small. Particularly good in any garden for autumn colour, producing fabulous red, orange and yellow leaves. Shelter from cold winds. Likes sun or partial shade and well-drained soils. H 1m (3ft), S 1.5m (5ft).

Acer pseudoplatanus 'Brilliantissimum' (sycamore)
A real showstopper in spring when its leaves emerge a brilliant orange salmony pink, then turn yellow and finally a dark green. It's not fussy about conditions but will do best in sun and well-drained soil. H 6m (20ft), S 8m (26ft).

Arbutus unedo (Killarney strawberry tree)
This has beautiful, rough, brown bark and bears urn-shaped white flowers in autumn as well as interesting fruit that look like strawberries. It's an evergreen with glossy, deep green leaves. Prefers sun and fertile, well-drained soil. H and S 8m (26ft).

Group of *Betula* trees underplanted with *Eragrostis curvula* (love grass).

Betula utilis var. jacquemontii
(West Himalayan birch)
I use birch a lot – I love their white trunks. Plant them in groups of three or more to create a small woodland area. As they don't cast a lot of shade, they can be underplanted with spring bulbs, for example, snowdrops and bluebells. They look great against black or dark green fences. They like moist, well-drained soil and an open, sunny position. H 15m (50ft), S 7m (25ft). For the smaller garden, *Betula pendula* 'Youngii' (Young's weeping birch) is a better bet. H 8m (26ft), S 10m (30ft).

Carpinus betulus 'Fastigiata'
(hornbeam)
The perfect street tree. It has a very distinctive, pyramidal, graceful shape and is excellent for structural divisions within the garden. It likes an open site and sunny, well-drained soil. A deciduous tree with good autumn colours. H 10m (30ft), S 12m (40ft).

Catalpa bignonioides
(Indian bean tree)
This deciduous tree is grown for its foliage and flowers. The leaves are really big and heart-shaped and the flowers, which are a bit like those of a horse chestnut, arrive in July and August. Likes a sunny position in moist soil and shelter from strong winds. H and S 15m (50ft).

Cercis canadensis 'Forest Pansy'
(Eastern redbud)
Deciduous with enchanting, heart-shaped, deep red-purple leaves. Great as a specimen tree for a smaller area. Tolerates dappled shade and likes a deep, fertile, moisture-retentive soil. H and S 10m (30ft).

Cordyline australis 'Atropurpurea'
(New Zealand cabbage palm)
This is a bit tender to frost, so not ideal for everywhere, but is great for creating a tropical look. A small tree, usually forming a single trunk with several branches, each topped by a large, dense mass of long, purple, sword-like leaves – a bit like a phormium. A great mass of creamy-white flowers is produced in big bunches in early summer. Grow in fertile, well-drained soil and full light or partial shade. H 5m (16ft), S 2m (6ft).

Crataegus laevigata 'Paul's Scarlet'
(hawthorn)
Great for a small garden. Deciduous tree with pinkish-scarlet flowers from late spring to summer. Attractive, dark green, toothed leaves. Prefers sunny, well-drained soil. Good in coastal, exposed or polluted areas. H 7m (23ft), S 8m (25ft).

Eucalyptus perriniana (silver dollar gum)
Fast growing evergreen with grey-blue leaves and grey and brown peeling bark. Grow in fertile, well-drained soil and provide shelter from cold winds. If it grows too big, you can prune it hard and it will start growing again. H 7m (23ft), S 5m (15 ft).

Ginkgo biloba (maidenhair tree)
This tree has been around for millions of years. In fact, it was probably something dinosaurs snacked on. It's as tough as old boots and is reputed to be the first thing that started growing on the wastelands of Hiroshima after the atomic bomb. It is one of the few deciduous conifers – its unusual-shaped leaves go a delectable buttery yellow in autumn. In addition, it has aphrodisiac properties – what more can you ask of a tree? Good on moist, well-drained soil and in sun or semi-shade. Ideal as a specimen tree in a large garden. H 15m (50ft), S 8m (26ft).

Hamamelis mollis (Chinese witch hazel)
If you have acid soil, you're lucky because you can grow this beauty. It's deciduous with extremely fragrant, yellow flowers strap-shaped petals in autumn to early spring. Likes moist soil in full sun or partial shade. H and S 4m (13ft).

Liquidambar styraciflua (sweet gum)
This is an amazing specimen tree for a large garden. It has a beautiful shape in outline and its leaves turn magnificent shades of orange and crimson in the autumn. Grow in fertile, moist but well-drained soil. Will tolerate semi-shade. H 25m (80ft), S 18m (60ft).

PLANTING TREES

- In general, trees will establish much better if planted while very young. They also have the advantage of being cheap and may not need staking or protection.
- Trees are one of the groups of plants that will benefit from watering through times of stress in their first few years as they lose an enormous amount of water through their foliage and sometimes find it difficult to replace.
- Many trees can be successfully grown for a long period in containers as long as the surface soil at the base of the tree is top dressed on a regular basis.
- Always consider the eventual height and spread of a specimen before planting. There's nothing more heartbreaking than having to remove an established tree because it has outgrown its allotted space. A tree when mature should ideally be no more than two-thirds the height of your house.
- When staking a tree, be careful to leave ample room for the girth to expand and not be strangled by the tree tie.
- As a general rule, the optimum ratio of deciduous to evergreen trees and shrubs in the garden is 70:30. While evergreens are great for providing permanent colour throughout the winter, they do need to be balanced by the changing colours and shapes of the deciduous trees.

Prunus (cherry)

I know cherry trees really do their thing for only a few weeks in spring, but they're worth it. In their native land, Japan, the entire country goes into fiesta mode for these few weeks and every day the newspapers carry bulletins charting the blossom front line, which sweeps upwards through Japan from the tropical south to the arctic north. My favourites are *Prunus yedoensis* (Yoshino cherry) with spreading branches and white or pale pink, almond-scented flowers (H 8.5m/26ft, S 10m/33ft) and 'Taihaku' (great white cherry), which has gorgeous, white, fragrant blossoms (H 8m/26ft, S 10m/33ft). *Prunus serrula* has beautiful, gleaming, coppery-red bark that you can actually polish with a soft rag (H and S 10m/33ft), and the leaves of 'Shirotae' turn orange-red in autumn (H 8m/25ft, S 10m/33ft). Cherries grow in any well-drained soil in the sun.

Robinia pseudoacacia 'Frisia' (false acacia)

The colour of this tree is quite startling – it has very bright yellow-green leaflets, which makes it really stand out from the crowd. It will grow in anything but water-logged soil. Prefers to be in the sun – don't we all? H 15m (50ft), S 8m (26ft).

The double deep pink blossom of *Prunus* 'Kanzan' (flowering cherry).

Sorbus 'Joseph Rock' (mountain ash)

This is really an all-year-round performer. White flowers in early spring are followed in autumn by big clusters of yellow fruit which remain on the tree well after leaf fall. The leaves provide wonderful autumnal colours in tints of purple, copper and scarlet. Grow in sunny, fertile, moisture-retentive soil. H 10m (33ft), S 7m (23ft).

Taxus baccata 'Fastigiata' (yew)

Not only good for graveyards – this columnar variety is brilliant for architectural planting. Beware, though, of the highly poisonous red fruits if you have kids. Tolerates very dry and shady conditions. H 5–8m (16–26ft), S 2–3m (6–10ft).

SHRUBS Many of your garden's needs can be met using shrubs: hedging, screening, softening structures, edging, filling in gaps and creating mixed borders.

For the first few years when I was landscaping in Dublin and producing new gardens at the rate of eight to ten a year, the trick was to get the job done. This sometimes inhibited learning and creativity. The gardens began to contain many echoes of each other. It is a very easy trap to fall into and this was very apparent on my plant-buying trips. Do you remember that advert for the Milk Marketing Board? Chirpy milkman, 5 in the morning, drives his milk float down suburban street. The milk bottles hop out and line up behind him. Off he marches, bottles bouncing in his wake. He barks instructions and three toddle up to Mrs Brown's door and four to the Smiths'. The empties make an orderly way back to the van. Well, it was a little bit like that in the garden centre for me. I'd drive in, park the van and it would appear that it filled itself up with the usual suspects. They had hopped over the beds and borders while I wasn't looking and settled themselves nice and snugly into the back of my van. As I drove off they'd keep deadly quiet, but as soon as I arrived on to the job, I could almost hear them laughing gleefully

Above Cotoneaster horizontalis **is a faithful garden stalwart.**

together – the same old bunch were back again for another excursion. And that old bunch contained the ones that I knew I could rely on to build up a pretty picture. Some of the bunch are now old favourites.

Buddleia davidii (butterfly bush)
Butterflies love it, suburbia can't live without it and it has wheedled its way into many of the gardens I have planted. 'Black Knight' has dark green leaves, which are soft and white underneath, and bears heavy clusters of fragrant, dark violet-purple flowers from mid-summer. It's deciduous and likes full sun and well-drained soil. H and S 5m (15ft).

Buxus sempervirens (box)
No gardener's bag of tricks is complete without this one. Useful for formal hedges and topiary. Small, dark green leaves. Sun or semi-shade and anything but waterlogged soil. H and S 5m (15ft).

Cotinus coggygria 'Royal Purple' (smoke bush)
A striking and luxuriant shrub with deep wine-purple leaves. The flowers form cloudy, deep pink plumes in summer. Best in full sun. Deciduous. H and S 5m (15ft).

Dodonaea viscosa 'Purpurea'
Evergreen shrub grown mainly for its shimmery, coppery-purple foliage. It is somewhat tender to frost and prefers full sun and well-drained soil. H 2.5m (8ft), S 1.5m (5ft).

Euonymus fortunei 'Emerald Gaiety'
A very old, faithful friend. Bushy with white-edged, deep green leaves, sometimes with the faintest flush of pink. Great ground cover and all-year interest. Sun or semi-shade, well-drained soil. Evergreen. H 1m (3ft), S 1.5m (5ft).

Fatsia japonica
This evergreen looks a bit like a house plant and it can sometimes be damaged by frost. Very large, polished, dark green, palmate leaves give a wonderful, tropical effect. Globular, greenish-cream flower heads in October. Will do well in sun or shade and is excellent for seaside gardens. H 3m (10ft), S 3m (10ft).

Hydrangea arborescens 'Annabelle'
A showy and glamorous plant. It is deciduous with spectacular, large, rounded heads of white flowers in summer. Likes semi-shade and moist but well-drained soil. H and S 2.5m (8ft).

PLANTING SHRUBS

- With shrubs look for a good specimen. This will generally mean a bushy plant. Tip it out of its pot while still in the garden centre and see that a good root structure has formed. Buy common shrubs in groups of three and let them mound together.
- Remember to choose a balance between deciduous and evergreen.
- Some shrubs such as *Sarcococca* may appear to be boring but don't be deceived – the beauty lies not so much in what is seen but what it smells like when in flower.
- Water the shrub before you plant it and again after you have planted it. Then water a couple more times in the first week or two but after that let it search itself for water – this will encourage the roots to grow.

Lavandula augustifolia 'Munstead' (lavender)

Evergreen, bushy shrub with dense spikes of fragrant, blue flowers from mid- to late summer and narrow, aromatic, silver-grey leaves. As a Mediterranean plant, it does best in full sun with well-drained soil. Also good by the sea. *Lavandula stoechas* (French lavender) is less hardy but has really stunning purple flowers. H and S 60cm (2ft).

Melianthus major (honeybush)

A tropical and delicate-looking plant. This shrub is evergreen but is hardy only in the mildest of areas. In colder areas it will act like a herbaceous plant, dying over winter and returning in the spring. It has greeny, bluey, greyish leaves, which are long and deeply toothed. Requires sun and well-drained soil. H and S 2–3m (6–10ft).

Nandina domestica 'Firepower' (sacred bamboo)

Looks a bit like a bamboo, and is evergreen or semi-evergreen. The foliage is yellow-green in summer and orange-red when young and in the winter. Place it in a sheltered position in sun or shade in any well-drained soil. H 1m (3ft), S 60cm (2ft).

Pachysandra terminalis (Japanese spurge)

This is a very useful, dwarf, evergreen, creeping shrub – it's useful because it's great for carpeting awkward areas under trees as it loves dark shade. Tiny, white flowers in early summer. H 10cm (4in), S 20cm (8in).

Prunus laurocerasus 'Otto Luyken' (common or cherry laurel)

This one's a real hard slogger. You can put it virtually anywhere, in sun or shade, and it will perform. It's an evergreen with dark green leaves and spikes of white flowers in the spring. H 1m (3ft), S 2m (6ft).

Rosmarinus officinalis 'Miss Jessopp's Upright' (rosemary)

This plant has much to offer – it's evergreen, easy to grow, has blue flowers in spring and sometimes again in autumn and can be used as a culinary herb. It likes sun and well-drained soil. H and S 2m (6ft).

Santolina chamaecyparissus 'Lemon Queen' (cotton lavender)

Crush the foliage to release its delicious smell. Evergreen, rounded, dense shrub. Shoots are covered with woolly, white

growth and finely toothed leaves. Lemon-yellow flower heads in mid- to late summer. Needs sun and not too rich, well-drained soil. H 75cm (2ft 6in), S 1m (3ft).

Sarcococca confusa (Christmas box)
This one's definitely for the front garden because it comes into flower in the depths of winter when you probably won't be out the back much. Plant it along the path to your front door and enjoy the delicious wafts of scent as you brush past it. It earns its keep for the rest of the year

too as an attractive, glossy evergreen. Grows in sun or shade in well-drained soil. H and S 1m (3ft).

Viburnum davidii
Not the most exciting plant ever but eternally useful as it is a good-looking evergreen and does well in sun or shade. Dome-shaped and compact, with tiny, white flowers in spring. Ask for a mixture of male and female plants to get the plants to make fruit – attractive, metallic-looking blue berries. H 80cm (2ft 9in), S 1.5m (5ft).

This combination of foliage contains real drama. Euphorbia, bamboo, *Eriobotrya japonica* and banana all vie for attention.

Yucca filamentosa (Adam's needle)
Yuccas are dramatic evergreens, with dagger-like, stiff, upright leaves edged with fine hairs. They are arid and exotic-looking, evocative of Californian deserts. In summer, a surprise comes in the form of a spire of delicate creamy-white, bell-shaped flowers which rise up from the centre. Needs sun and well-drained soil. H 2m (6ft), S 1.5m (5ft).

SHOWSTOPPERS
Just one special plant can enliven a sobre planting plan, add a touch of glamour to a family garden or perfectly punctuate a minimalist design.

This is a very personal choice. Not everybody likes the same show tunes. And, of course, the choice changes from week to week if not day by day. I like to celebrate these plants in a garden, to have them noticed. But mainly I want to see them as I walk around. If you have limited space, they inject interest and drama. If you have a spare, minimalist garden, you will need an exciting plant to stop it looking just boring. From the galaxy of plants, here are my stars.

Canna 'Assaut'
This is a remarkable plant. It has lush, purple-green foliage with dazzling, scarlet flowers in summer. Very showy and Caribbean, but tender to frost. Requires a warm, sunny position and moist soil. H to 1.2m (4ft), S 45–60cm (1ft 6in–2ft).

Cupressus sempervirens (Italian cypress)
Tall, slender and evocative of rolling Tuscany countryside, this tree provides dramatic, vertical interest when you wish to lead the eye skywards. Best in a warm, sunny site with shelter from cold winds. H 15m (50ft), S 5m (15ft).

Dicksonia antarctica
(Tasmanian tree fern)
This is one of my all-time favourite plants and I use it a lot when creating gardens. It is elegant and dramatic and gives instant jungle effect. It requires very little looking after – just spray the fronds with a gentle mist of water in the summer and cut off any dead fronds in the spring. Contrary to its tropical appearance, it is actually hardy in most of the British Isles as it comes from the mountains of Tasmania where temperatures can plunge far below zero. Likes semi-shade and rich, moist soil. H 10m (30ft), S 4m (12ft). Less commonly known but equally beautiful is *Cyathea australis* (Australian tree fern) whose leaves are bluish underneath. If in a very dry area, wrap stem with moss and drench. Moss will retain a lot of water during dry spells and will act as protection against frost in the winter. H 8m (25ft), S 5m (15ft).

Gunnera manicata (giant prickly rhubarb/poor man's umbrella)
If you want a plant that really makes a statement, look no further than gunnera. But you do need adequate space for this plant as its outlandishly large leaves up to 1.5m (5ft) across can dwarf plants and places. It has compound flower heads in summer, the overall outline of which is like a cone. It likes moist and rich soil, semi-shade, shelter from wind and a position in or beside water. It is not completely hardy in Britain – the trick is to protect its crown over winter by covering it with its own dying leaves. H 2m (6ft), S 2.2m (7ft).

Magnolia campbellii 'Charles Raffill'
For purely seasonal glamour, like that of the *haute couture* shows in Paris, Milan and London, nothing can compare to a magnolia in full flower. Even though they are the supermodels of the plant catwalk, they are surprisingly low-maintenance. 'Charles Raffill' has lipstick-pink, outrageously big, fragrant flowers in spring. Likes sun and well-drained soil. H 16m (52ft), S 11m (35ft). Another beauty is *Magnolia wilsonii*, with beautiful, white, fragrant flowers, suitable for the smaller garden. H 8m (26ft), S 6m (20ft).

Musa basjoo (banana tree)
While it won't actually produce any edible bananas for you, this tree will certainly create atmosphere of the tropical rainforest variety. However, it is not terribly hardy, so use only in sheltered

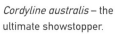

Cordyline australis – the
ultimate showstopper.

Add a touch of the tropical rainforests to your garden with *Dicksonia antarctica* – one of my all-time favourites.

bamboo leaves transports you to far-away, tranquil places. H 6–8m (20–26ft), S indefinite. Also try *Phyllostachys aurea*.

Stipa gigantea (giant oat grass)
It's quite magical when the early morning or evening sun lights up this plant. It's like having a small slice of farming countryside in your garden. Place in a sunny position and well-drained soil. H 2.5m (8ft), S 1m (3ft). Grasses, in general, are great. They are easy to care for and look good most of the year round. They are fashionable at the moment. Other grasses I would recommend are *Stipa arundinacea* (pheasant grass)(H 1.5m /5ft, S 1.2m/4ft), *Miscanthus sinensis* (H 1.2m/4ft, S 45cm/1½ ft), *Cortaderia selloana* (pampas grass) (H 2.5m/8ft, S 1.2m/4ft) and *Helictotrichon sempervirens* (blue oat grass) (H 1m/3ft, S 60cm/2ft).

Trachycarpus fortunei (chusan/windmill palm)
This is an evergeen, summer-flowering palm. It has a lovely hairy trunk, big fan-shaped leaves up to 1.2m (4ft) across and big, drooping clusters of flowers. Amazingly hardy and wonderfully exotic. It does prefer shelter from cold, dry winds. Grow in sun and fertile, well-drained soil. H 10m (30ft), S 2.5m (8ft).

places and wrap the base of the stem with straw or plastic to keep warm in the winter. Likes sun and well-drained soil. H 3–5m (10–15ft), S 2–2.5m (6–8ft).

Phormium tenax (New Zealand flax)
This is the full stop in garden punctuation. It has beautiful form and comes in some really stunning purple hues. It will add a touch of the exotic to any garden and does particularly well in seaside locations. Likes sun and moist but well-drained soil but can be frost tender. If damaged by frost, cut out the whole of

the damaged frond, otherwise it can rot down and damage all of the plant. Protect by wrapping in hessian, fleece or straw over the winter. H 3m (10ft), S 1–2m (3–6ft).

Phyllostachys nigra (black bamboo)
Very trendy at the moment, but don't let that put you off. Evergreen and clump-forming with black stems. Likes sun and well-drained soil. Use bamboos to form instant screens for privacy or to create boundaries within your garden. And when the wind blows, the rustling of

HERBACEOUS PLANTS Here are my top twenty must-have herbaceous plants, the all-singing, all-dancing plants of the garden.

Herbaceous plants inject colour, variety and smiles into your borders. They die down in winter, but don't panic: you haven't killed them – they re-emerge in the spring. For this reason, it can be a good idea to plant them with winter- and spring-flowering bulbs, which will fill the bare patches in the border until the herbaceous plants come on stage again.

Acanthus mollis (bear's breeches)
Often described as architectural and for good reason – its leaves are large and bold and it produces statuesque, sturdy spikes of mauve and white flowers. Prefers the sun but will tolerate shade and likes well-drained soil. H 1.2m (4ft), S 45cm (1ft 6in).

Agapanthus africanus (African lily)
Deep blue flowers and a simple beauty. Tender to frost, so protect the base over winter. Likes full sun and moist but well-drained soil. H 1m (3ft), S 50cm (1ft 8in).

Alchemilla mollis (lady's mantle)
A little gurrier – gets in everywhere. It is beautiful and unusual as its flowers are green. Tries to shout at you a number of times during the season by flowering frequently and in rain it's just fantastic because of the beads of water that lodge on its hairy leaves. Grow in sun or partial shade. H and S 50cm (1ft 8in).

Astilbe arendsii 'Fanal'
Crimson-red plumes of flowers that manage to remain good looking even when they die in autumn. Likes semi-shade and damp soil, so another good one for the waterside. H 60cm (2ft), S to 1m (3ft).

Astrantia major (masterwort)
Papery-looking flowers in pink, white and green which last quite a long time over the summer. Lends an informal, meadowy feel to planting. Likes sun or semi-shade and well-drained soil. H 60cm (2ft), S 45cm (1ft 6in).

Cimicifuga simplex (bugbane)
When many perennials have packed their bags and gone off to hibernate, cimicifuga comes out to play. Arching spires of tiny, slightly fragrant, star-shaped, white flowers in autumn and very dark leaves. Likes semi-shade and moist conditions. H 1.2m (4ft), S 60cm (2ft).

Crocosmia 'Lucifer' (montbretia)
Brilliant fiery-red flowers will warm up cold spots. Likes a well-drained soil in an open, sunny site. H to 1m (3ft), S 20–25cm (8–10in).

Achillea millefolium 'Cerise Queen' – another stunning herbaceous plant not to be overlooked.

Plant *Kniphofia* in drifts to create maximum impact.

Dicentra spectabilis (bleeding heart)
The first time you see this plant, you will be amazed at the shape of the pink and white flowers – perfectly formed like a heart-shaped locket. A real gem. Enjoys semi-shade and moist but well-drained soil. H 75cm (2ft 6in), S 50cm (1ft 8in).

Digitalis purpurea (foxglove)
Reminder of bygone days. Foliage as soft as fabric. Silvery green leaves and flowers that know they are dramatic but are slightly lazy with it. The flowers in summer can vary from pink and purple to white. They grow in most conditions but prefer semi-shade and moist but well-drained soil. H 1.1–2.2m (4–7ft), S 60cm (2ft).

Geranium 'Johnson's Blue'
A real trouper. Traditional and useful. Grows in all soils and isn't too bothered about sun and shade. A romantic. H 30cm (1ft), S 60cm (2ft).

Hemerocallis (day lily)
A plant that smiles at you. The flowers last only a day, hence the common name daylily, but they open in rapid succession. Many colours are available and the foliage looks good too when the flowers disappear. Full sun or partial shade and moist soil, so a good choice for the waterside. H and S vary according to variety but approximate H 30cm–1m (1–3ft).

Heuchera micrantha 'Palace Purple'
Attracts vine weevil all too readily, so check all purchases very, very carefully. The deep purple leaves spell a luxury much the same as good chocolate. Prefers semi-shade and moist but well-drained soil. H and S 45cm (1ft 6in).

Hosta (plantain lily)
Sharp plants with acres of foliage that gardeners and slugs adore. Also produce decorative spikes of flowers. They are hardy, highly adaptable and require little care. Prefer partial shade and moist soil and are good waterside plants. Great range of cultivars with foliage from very grey-blue to bright yellow, some with decorative margins. H from 2.5cm (1in) to 1m (3ft) and S from 30cm to 1.5m (5ft).

Iris sibirica (Siberian flag) and *Iris pseudacorus* (yellow flag)
Startling jewels of colour on sword-like stems. Absurdly beautiful and easy. Good in moist soil, particularly on the margins of a garden pool. *Iris sibirica* produces blue-purple flowers. H 50cm–1.2m (1ft 8in–4ft). *Iris pseudacorus* has golden-yellow flowers and prefers semi-shade. H 2m (6ft).

Ligularia dentata 'Desdemona'
This belongs to the shady, waterside repertoire. It has big, brown, leathery leaves and cheerful, orange daisy flowers on the end of tall stems in summer. H 1.2m (4ft), S 60cm (2ft).

Nepeta faassenii (catmint)
Purple exuberance that cats and bees love – both are attracted to the aromatic foliage. Often used as edging on a border. Sun or partial shade. H and S 45cm (1ft 6in).

Rudbeckia fulgida var. *deamii* (black-eyed Susan)
A very happy plant – lots of colourful, yellow, daisy-like flowers with black centres that last into autumn. Likes sun or shade and well-drained or moist soil. H 1m (3ft), S 60cm (2ft).

Sedum spectabile 'Brilliant' (ice-plant)
Flat heads of small, pink flowers that appear from late summer to autumn. Good for a wildlife garden – butterflies love this plant. Requires sun and well-drained soil. H and S 30–45cm (1ft–1ft 6in).

Verbascum 'Gainsborough' (mullein)
Tall, elegant spires to provide vertical interest in a border. Pale yellow flowers on spikes throughout summer. Tolerates shade but prefers to be in the sun. H 1.2m (4ft), S 30–60cm (1–2ft).

Verbena bonariensis
Tall stems with small, mauve flowers on top for many months in the summer and autumn. Will seed freely and is quite informal-looking. Sunshine and free-draining soil required. H 1.5m (5ft), S 60cm (2ft).

CASE STUDIES

LIGHTING

PLANTING

LAWNS

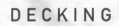

DECKING

WATER

LIVING SPACE

PLAY AREAS

STORAGE

BUILDINGS

POD A couple and their two children had lived in suburban Surrey for a few years. They were perfectly happy with the inside of their house, but felt that outside there was just a nightmare garden, for one important reason – it was on a slope, a very dramatic slope, with an abandoned, dangerous pond at the end of it.

THE DESIGN BRIEF

No area of the garden was usable other than a plain concrete slab patio directly outside the living room window, and if the children wanted to play outside they had to go to a friend's house to do it. Their parents weren't gardeners – they didn't mind looking after some plants but having hectic work, family and social lives they really wanted to spend their spare time enjoying their space rather than mowing a lawn. So, having noted that their four-year-old son had drawn a space rocket in his garden plan, I decided to add some humour and colour, but most of all to create a functional space at the back of the house that would answer the needs of all the family and conquer the challenge of a broad and forbidding, sloping site.

Levelling out and building decks on different areas of the steep hill created functional and easily maintainable platforms and essential outdoor family living areas.

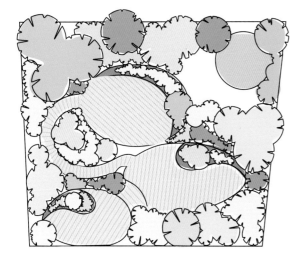

A space rocket acted as both a sculptural feature and a children's den. It was the surprise element at the bottom of the garden.

DESIGN SOLUTION

With such a steep hill to work with, levelling out the different areas by creating platforms seemed like the best option. Three decking areas in elliptical shapes were designed to create usable floor space stepped through the garden. The first deck led from the patio doors of the house and, beneath it, the two lower decks were supported by telegraph poles to make them appear as if they were floating. Each deck had steps leading from one to another. In order to keep the maple tree, which had a preservation order on it, the third decking platform was built around it. Decking is an easy and flexible medium to use and a comparatively inexpensive material.

Aubergine-coloured planters constructed from fibreglass were placed on each deck to serve as barriers to stop the children falling off. Fibreglass was a material that I had been dubious about for years; I remembered my brother repairing canoes in the family garage with the stuff and never felt it appropriate for garden construction. But because the planters were to be retro in feel and were inspired by, among other things, a bar at a night-club in San Francisco Airport, a material with flexible properties needed to be found. So eventually I came across Barry Storey of North Kent Moulders who hadn't a clue what he was letting himself in for. He ended up closing his

factory for three days and three nights to rush our requirements into production. Holes were drilled into the base of the planters for drainage, before each was filled with topsoil and compost, ready for planting.

The disused pond at the end of the garden was cleared and filled in with cement. In each of the planters, a small fountain was placed with a foam-effect nozzle to enhance the sound of the water. To protect the children, a metal grid was placed just under the surface of the fountain – this also prevents leaves from clogging up the pump.

Finally, their son got his space rocket. This was constructed from ribs of marine plywood and squares of galvanised aluminium. The rocket was inspired by years of viewing *Star Trek*, *Doctor Who* and *Flash Gordon*. It's reminiscent of the space race and Apollo 13 which we've all grown up hearing about. Access to the spaceship was in the form of a ready-made fibreglass slide which led from the third deck to the bottom of the garden. A mini forest of birch trees newly planted around the rocket and at the base of the decks visually linked the garden into a leafy green forest across the valley.

Most of the planting was contained in fibreglass planters. Plants could be rearranged at different times of the year and spot colour could be added occasionally. Jets of water amongst the beds created excitement.

PLANTING

The planting was sub-tropical and mainly reflected the kind of plants that the clients had admired when they visited the magnificent Palm House in Kew Gardens. These included tree ferns, palm trees, cannas, hardy varieties of banana plants and large bamboos.

I also used several low-maintenance plants such as heuchera, geranium, alchemilla, euonymus and pachysandra. The waist-high planters allow for easy gardening as there is no bending over involved.

CUBE
The client had just finished renovating his house in an ultra-modern, minimalist style and was keen for a garden that would complement the house – contemporary, sleek and using new materials which would reflect the interior of his home.

THE DESIGN BRIEF

The plot was a small, square, high-walled courtyard that led directly from the back of the house. It was completely bare – white walls, concrete and utterly devoid of any plant life. This is a great starting point for designing a garden as it has no previous associations and is an open space to be filled by your imagination. The client wanted an architectural, low-maintenance, modern garden, with only non-flowering plants. He also wanted the garden to be an outdoor place to retreat to and somewhere that would have a usable life which would extend beyond just the summer.

A glass cube suspended over a still, tiled pond created the perfect outdoor space. Traditionally, a structure like this would have been attached to the house but when set apart it becomes a place of true escape.

THE DESIGN SOLUTION

Taking inspiration from glass structures such as the pyramid at the Louvre in Paris and also observing how Damien Hirst was fond of framing life forms within glass, I decided to create a cube room completely of glass which would 'float' above water and act as an escape - a room within a garden. This acted as a cool and transparent seating area, a focal point for the garden and a point from which to view the rest of the garden. The cube was supported by an elegant metal grid, which was in turn supported by steel legs standing in the pond. To give the effect of the pond being deeper than it actually was, I lined it with black mosaic tiles – ideal in this situation. The internationally renowned fashion designer, John Rocha, was invited to add his touch, which turned out to be a simple and Zen-like wooden water feature.

Metal walkways were suspended over sunken bedding areas to give the feeling that you are actually walking over the planting. A white concrete walkway led from the back of the house to create the effect of a catwalk leading up to the pond. Blue glass lenses were inserted into the concrete which were lit from underneath at night. The white walls were painted a cobalt blue, which was

Exotics such as *Cordyline australis* 'Atropurpurea' and *Dicksonia antarctica* completed the subtropical feel.

chosen to complement the greenery of the planting. A square of gold painted on the wall seemed to add an Indian touch and reflected the overall shape of the garden. Finally, a small patio area was created, again in white concrete, with the addition of an outdoor heater to enable the owner to sit outside in the winter.

PLANTING

The owner was very clear about what he wanted – a rainforest feel, with minimal flower interest and, more importantly, minimal maintenance. To create this effect I used an abundance of ferns, such as *Cyrtomium fortunei*, *Dryopteris dilatata*, *Polystichum polyblepharum*, and introduced plenty of detail to the planting in order to add variety, texture and colour. We used Tasmanian tree ferns, *Dicksonia antarctica*, and the Chusan palm, *Trachycarpus fortunei*, to provide instant drama and tropical effect. A lot of plants were chosen for their fondness of shade. As well as the ferns, Japanese anemones, *Geranium phaeum*, Astrantia and various types of grasses also fall into this category. The cube provided a perfect glasshouse for such tender beauties as the umbrella grass. The fact that the garden is well protected against the wind by high walls meant that we were able to plant some banana plants, *Musa basjoo*. The Italian conifers were used to add height and to draw the eye upwards.

SHARK Long, narrow, boring and overlooked by the neighbours: this was a fairly typical suburban garden in need of a radical transformation and restructuring – not the impossible task it may seem at first.

DESIGN BRIEF

The owner of this garden had a problem. She had a quite a large plot but, as she lived in the middle of flatland, her garden was overlooked by both the upper flat of the house she lived in and by a multitude of neighbours. It had no features other than a lonely shed way down the end and a nearby apple tree. The garden consisted of wall-to-wall lawn, a concrete path and a slab patio directly outside the glass doors. She was interested in gardening and really wanted to make the best of this large space. Her main requirement was for a garden in two sections – one with a new paved area, lawn and borders and another much more private situation that she could enjoy on her own, or with her friends.

DESIGN SOLUTION

To achieve the desired effect I decided to divide the garden two thirds of the way down and create a private area beyond a large structure. The top two thirds of the garden were shaped into a most elegant, if somewhat unconventional, area of

lawns and borders. The main lawn was shaped like a leaf – almost two sharp curves meeting each other. A second lawn was simply put in at a slightly lower level and these two areas of green acted as a foil against all the planting and every other surface. Decking was used up near the top of the house as the owner was a barefoot person and liked to wander straight from her living room into the garden. The first lawn cut into the deck quite dramatically.

The garden was then divided by a towering steel structure in the shape of a shark's fin. The idea behind this was to achieve the desired effect of privacy in at least one area of the garden whilst not creating a wall the whole way across the garden. Using a shape such as a shark's fin introduced a sculptural element as well as drama and humour. In front of the structure I created a pond which was designed to mirror the fin, both in terms of shape and reflection. Visitors to the garden would be restricted to this area while being enticed by a submarine door-type opening in the steel. Through this doorway was a tantalising glimpse of a

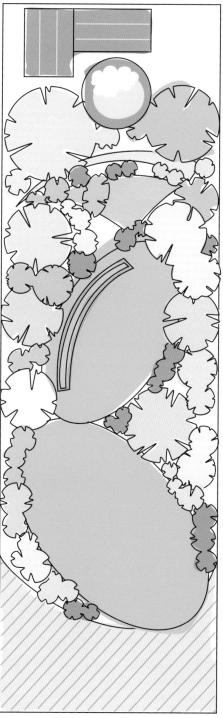

personal paradise beyond. This was to be the owner's personal space which would be an area where she could spend time alone and in privacy.

As the ultimate luxury, a heated spa pool was installed into this furthest part of the garden. By recessing it into the ground to a depth of 30cm, I was able to plant the surrounding walls and blend it naturally into this new, lush, tropical paradise.

Page 153 A traditional lawn set on two levels surrounded by both mixed borders and dramatic planting leads down to a steel structure in the form of a shark's fin. The fin acts as both a focal point and a garden divider to entice the visitor but also hides a secondary garden beyond.

Opposite A spa pool and outdoor shower furnish a contemporary Garden of Eden.

Right The submarine-type opening in the shark fin frames a view back up the garden to the house.

To create a comfortable space for changing into swimwear for the hot tub I extented the existing 10ft by 8ft shed by simply attaching a new 6ft by 4ft shed to it. This new building also provided the perfect housing for the electrical fusebox to power the hot tub. Both sheds were then painted the same dark blue colour as the surrounding fences which made them blend in both to each other and the background.

PLANTING

The aspect was good, open and sunny and yet sheltered so I had a large choice of plants available to me. The theme for planting was to be traditional meets tropical, so herbaceous plants would melt into cannas, tree ferns and palms. Tropical effects were achieved by using Tasmanian tree ferns *Dicksonia antarctica*, the grass tree *Xanthorrhoea*, *Canna tropicana* and *Trachycarpus fortunei*. The shark's fin was settled into the garden and softened by this planting. Elsewhere around the garden planting was more traditional. In contrast to the exotic bed, I planted what nearly amounted to a herbaceous border at the top of the garden near the deck, using *Ligularia przewalskii*, *Jubaea chilensis*, silver Artemesia and a host of different grasses including *Carex* 'Silver Sceptre', *Carex* 'Evergold', *Carex flagellifera* and *Carex* 'Frosted Curls'. Blue and white Agapanthus looked very striking against the navy fence. The spa pool was settled into the garden by planting a group of purple bananas, *Musa murelli*, *Hosta* 'Thomas Hogg' and *Heuchera* 'Palace Purple'. Mature specimens of *Rhus typhina*, *Betula pendula*, *Salix* and *Eucalyptus gunnii* helped shade the owner from her neighbours and gave a distinctively tropical feel to her private garden.

LAWN Lawns can sometimes be boring, flat and unexciting. But they don't have to be. This site provided an opportunity to create intrigue and interest in the garden by changing the lawn into some unusual shapes and undulations.

DESIGN BRIEF

The garden was a traditional, long, thin, rectangular shape with mature shrubs on either side of the lawn – a very typical suburban plot. The couple who lived here with their two children wanted a change. There was nothing wrong with the garden, *per se*, except that it was boring and they wanted something more exciting which better reflected their design taste and lifestyle. The sun set at the back of the garden and they wanted to have a sloped area to lie back on and relax with a drink as the sun went down.

DESIGN SOLUTION

To create different levels in the garden and interest in a flat, straight area, I created two hilly mounds – a bit like Teletubby land – which curved in an S shape through the garden. This immediately introduced mystery to the garden as it was not possible to view the whole garden from either end – you had to go and explore it. This made it a fun place for the children to run around in.

The contours also transformed the ordinary lawn into a contemporary living sculpture. But it's not that easy to mow a sculpture so this design wouldn't be for everyone but it appealed to our clients' wish for something a little bit different.

An oval-shaped, cave-like room was set into the hill at the end of the garden to provide a den for the children or an underground cage for late-night drinking. A heater was installed to make it usable on colder evenings. The oval opening of the cave door was echoed by a shallow, shimmering oval pool, which was constructed very simply from concrete.

Lighting effects were a big feature in this garden and were used to highlight structures and plants and create a magical and completely different garden by night. The cave was lit with a mysterious pink, various hues of blue spots were set along the banks of the hill, green floodlights underlit the shrubbery while the foliage at the outer edge of the borders was illuminated with blue lighting.

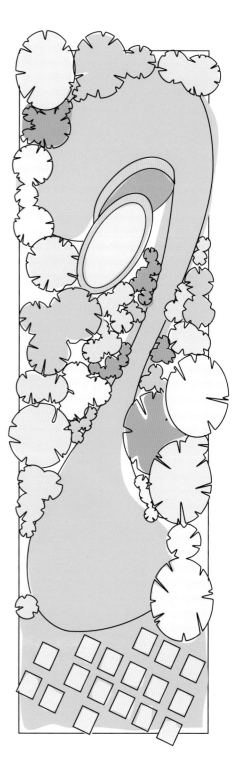

Left The cave was built as a retreat and is not visible from the house, so it reveals itself as a surprise destination at the end of your hill-walking!

Opposite A mysterious and complex mound snakes its way down the length of the garden, wrapping itself around the bubbling pool and finally swamps the roof of an outdoor room. Conventional, it's not.

The lawn area leading up to the house was then linked to the house by the use of concrete slabs which were set into the lawn in a grid fashion at an angle to the house. The angle served to tempt you into the garden to have a look around the next curve.

PLANTING

The existing planting around the perimeter of the garden was well-established and doing a good job so it remained. The main planting here was of course grass. But we're not just talking about the lawn; hundreds of ornamental grasses were used throughout the garden. These were planted in drifts of the same species. Grasses provide form, texture and movement and they also look good all year round so they are the perfect low maintenance plants.

The grasses chosen were varied both in their colour and in their form – the white variety of *Phalaris* 'Feesey', the grey-blue stiff tufts of *Helictotrichon sempervirens*, the orange-brown of *Stipa arundinacea* , the feathery *Stipa tenuissima* and the arching blue-green of *Miscanthus sinensis* 'Malepartus'. We also used different types of sedges such as *Carex comans* 'Bronze Form' and *Carex* 'Silver Sceptre'. Birches and laurels were used to soften the edges of the hills.

TRAY Creating different levels in a garden will give interest and movement to an otherwise large, flat expanse. In this garden I created three tiers which appeared to float above each other.

DESIGN BRIEF

The garden was large, broad, south-facing and very neglected. While the owners could see it had a lot of potential, they didn't know what do to with it. They did know that they wanted a carpentry workshop and also some privacy from the next door neighbours, but beyond that it was a big, blank canvas.

Three massive containers were constructed which appeared to hover over each other and create different levels of lawn and planting. The design was trying to create an illusion of defying gravity. The levels were underlit with blue neon at night to enhance the floating effect.

The stems of the birch trees are framed in a rectangle of stainless steel. Aluminium and stainless steel provide reflective surfaces for the birch stems which emerge from the ground underneath, and to mirror-image the garden as a whole on the side of the workshop.

DESIGN SOLUTION

The design solution was very linear and contained echoes of Frank Lloyd Wright's architecture, especially inspired by his house 'Falling Water', which has gravity defying balconies hovering above the water. The elements in the garden were a carpenter's studio at the very back and three main trays of floating gardens at different levels. The trays were rectangular, clad with stainless steel and designed to appear to virtually float above ground. Water flowed in extremely shallow, stainless steel rills through the trays and then dropped through letterbox-style openings in sheer turf into uncovered square ponds below.

The owner wanted a large workshop, but I didn't want it to dominate the garden so I sunk it three feet down into the ground. The underground part of the studio was a concrete floor, built up with solid blocks, and then the upper part was finished off as a wooden structure. Some areas of the top of the studio had corrugated perspex in the roof to allow for natural light. To give a contemporary and beautiful finish, the exterior of the structure was clad in aluminium squares which had circular discs in relief.

Night lighting was a big feature of this garden. Blue neon was used underneath the trays to emphasise their elevated and floating nature. Finally, a curvy concrete bench was made by concrete artist Rachel Reynolds to complement the linear lines of the planting and trays.

PLANTING

We used a mix of traditional and modern plants to both soften and highlight the strong, architectural feel of the garden. In particular, we made generous use of silver birch, and other plants requested by the clients such as a rectangular grove of Japanese maple, ferns, lavenders, yuccas, eucalyptus – all planted in square or rectangular blocks, highlighting the rectangular design of the garden. Three white-stemmed birches appeared to rise from a stainless steel square opening in one of the trays. Mixed borders of shrubs and herbaceous perennials included yuccas, cordyline, kniphofia, sedum and achillea. Bamboos provide a good instant screen so black bamboo, *Phyllostachys nigra*, was planted liberally along the fence.

SUPPLIERS

BUILDING MATERIALS

Ardex UK Ltd
Homefield Road, Haverhill,
Suffolk CB9 8QP
01440 714939

Asphaltic Roofing Supplies Ltd
Harding Way, St Ives,
Cambridgeshire PE17 4YJ
01480 466777
support@asphaltic.co.uk

B&Q
0800 444840

Camfaud Concrete Pumps Ltd
High Road, Thornwood Common,
Epping, Essex CM16 6LU
01992 560898

Castle Timber and Building
Materials Ltd
2a Bartholomew Road,
Kentish Town, London NW5 2NA
020 7428 0660

Concrete Pumping Coleshill Ltd
01675 464291

Hanson Premix London
231 Tunnel Avenue, North
Greenwich, London SE10 0QE
020 8269 4900

Jewsons
0800 539766

London Minimix
Townmead Road, London SW6 2QL
020 7731 7329

Nimblemix Ltd
Longside, Thorpe Lea Road, Egham,
Surrey TW20 8RH
01784 470071, fax 01784 470072

Noel Clay Ltd
Gin Close Way, Awsworth,
Nottinghamshire NG16 2TA
0115 938 2283, fax 0115 945 9270

RMC Aggregates Western
Wolverhampton Road,
Oldbury, West Midlands B69 4RJ
0121 552 6699

RMC Ready Mix Ltd
RMC House, High Street, Feltham,
Middlesex TW13 4HA
0800 667827, fax 020 8751 0006

RMD Quickform Midland Sales
Stubbors Green Road, Aldridge,
Walsall, West Midlands WS9 8BW
01922 743777

Rugby Cement
Crown House, Rugby, Warwickshire
CV21 2DT
01788 542111

Tarmac Central Ltd
Tunstad House, Buxton,
Derbyshire SK17 8TG
01298 768444

Travis Perkins
77 South Lambeth Road,
Vauxhall, London SW8 1RJ
020 7582 4255
08705 005500 for nearest branch

Perspex
Hamar Acrylics
238–240 Bethnal Green Road,
London E2 0AA
020 7739 2907, fax 020 7739 7807

Ineos Acrylics
PO Box 34, Duckworth Street,
Darwen, Lancashire BB3 1QB
01254 874444

Silicone sealant for windows
Evode Ltd
Anglo House, Scudmore Road,
Leicester LE3 1UQ
0116 232 2922

METAL GOODS

Baco Metal Centre
Birmingham New Road, Tipton,
West Midlands DY4 9AG
01902 431800, fax 01902 431899
also Fircroft Way, Edenbridge,
Kent TN8 6ES
01732 582700, fax 01732 582799

C F Sparrowhawk Ltd
24 Epsom Lane North,
Tadworth, Surrey KT20 5EH
01737 352889, fax 01737 371088

Elite Metalcraft
Unit 33 & 38, Silicon Business
Centre, 28 Wadsworth Road,
Perivale, Middlesex UB6 7JZ
020 8810 5122
www.elitemetalcraft.co.uk

Industrial Alloys Ltd
Unit 7, Tractor Spares Trading
Estate, Willenhall, West Midlands
WV13 3RS
01902 634000

Kent Manufacturing Wexford Ltd,
Ardcavan Works, Wexford, Ireland
00 353 5343216

Architectural wiremesh
Potter & Soar Ltd
Beaumont Road, Banbury,
Oxfordshire OX16 1SD
01295 253344, fax 01295 272132
www.wiremesh.co.uk
potter.soar@btinternet.com

Bike hoops
Glasdon Manufacturing Ltd
Industrial Estate, Poulton-le-Fielde,
Blackpool, Lancashire FY6 8JW
01253 891131

Butler sink frame
J&P Engineering
Old Pit Yard, Stanley, Ilkeston,
Derbyshire DE7 7HB
0115 944 0388 (also fax)
07768 317324

Domed tiles
James & Spackman
General Metal Spinning
Gibbons Brook, Sellindge, Ashford,
Kent TN25 6HH
01303 813723

Floating steel trays
Stuart Sharpless
Integrated Metal Solutions Ltd
17b Bakers Court, Paycocke Road,
Basildon, Essex SS14 3EH
01268 534133

Galvanized steel sheeting
Tip Top Trading
Unit 1, Cowley Mill Trading Estate,
Longbridge Way, Uxbridge,
Middlesex UB8 2YG
01895 258222

Metal frames
Boundary Metal Ltd
Building 195, New Greenham Park,
Newbury, Berkshire RG19 6HL
01635 42255, fax 01635 528432
peter@boundary-metal.co.uk

RSJ frame
PL Manufacturing
Unit 14, Cannon Business Park,
Gough Road, Coseley,
West Midlands WV14 8XR
01902 408515, fax 01902 497349

RSJ 'goal posts'
Adey Steel,
8 Sparrow Hill, Loughborough,
Leicestershire LE11 1BT
01509 556677

Semi-circular greenhouse
Semi-circular RSJs
The Angle Ring Company Ltd
Bloomfield Road, Tipton,
West Midlands DY4 9EH
0121 557 7241

Steel and aluminium sheets
C. Downhill Steels
Units C, D & E, Riverside Way,
Uxbridge, Middlesex UB8 2YS
01895 256681
www.downhills.co.uk

Steel leg supports for trays
Promet Technology Ltd
31 Chase Road, Park Royal,
London NW10 6PU
020 8965 3030

Steel security grill for pond
Molesey Metal Works
Island Farm Avenue, West Molesey,
Surrey KT8 2UZ
020 8979 1772

Support for glass cube
W & G Sissons Ltd
Carrwood Road, Sheepbridge,
Chesterfield, Derbyshire S41 9QB
01246 450255
www.sissons.co.uk

GLASS GOODS

Luxcrete
Premier House, Disraeli Road,
Park Royal, London NW10 7BT
020 8965 7292, fax 020 8961 6337

Glass windows and panels
Pilkington's UK Ltd
Prescott Road, St Helen's,
Merseyside WA10 3TT
01744 28882

MACHINERY AND EQUIPMENT HIRE/SUPPLY

Mini diggers
Caterpillar UK Ltd
0800 028 7778

Gordon Cork
Poplars Farm, County Lane, Codsall
Wood, Wolverhampton WV8 1RG
01902 842392
07970 451451

Grant Plant Ltd
Pioneer Works, Malvern Road,
Maidenhead, Berkshire SL6 7RD
01628 621161

Skips
Allen Skip Hire
Weaverhouse, 19–21 Chapel Road,
London SE27 0TP
020 7732 4684

Battleskips
020 8960 0302

United Wastecare
020 8874 8130
www.worldsendwaste.co.uk

Waste Cycle
Private Road No 4,
Colwick Industrial Estate,
Nottingham NG4 2JT
0115 940 3111

Wicksy's Skips
Gibbs Road, Edmonton, London
N18 3PU
020 8803 4394

Tool hire
Black & Decker
01753 511234

Bosch
01895 834466
www.bosch.co.uk

HSS
0845 728 2828

Lawson's Whetstone Ltd
1208 High Road, London N20 0LL
020 8446 1321, fax 020 8446 2509

Lynch Plant Hire and Haulage Ltd
Fourth Way, Wembley,
Middlesex HA9 0LH
020 8204 2244, fax 020 8900 9584

Robert Lee Plant Ltd
New Road Industrial Estate,
Hixon, Stafford ST18 0PJ
01889 271727, fax 01889 271728

Spear & Jackson
Neill Tools Ltd, Atlas Way, Atlas
North, Sheffield S4 7QQ
0114 281 4242

Speedy Hire Centre
Midlands – 01332 380493
Northern – 01744 697000
Southern – 01284 760842

Turf cutting machine
Kerb-line
7 Lampole House, Station Road,
Overton, Hampshire RG25 3TL
01256 773165

Wheelbarrows
Brandon Hire
53 Stafford Road, Wallington,
Surrey SM6 9AP
020 8669 5151
www.brandonhire.plc.uk

Haemmerlin
The Washington Centre,
Halesowen Road, Netherton,
West Midlands DY2 9RE
01384 243243

PAVING

Blanc de Bierges
Eastrea Road, Whittlesey,
Peterborough PE7 2AG
01733 202566
www.blancdebierges.com

Bradstones Home & Garden
Landscaping
Aggregates Industries UK Ltd,
Hulland Ward, Ashbourne,
Derbyshire DE6 3ET
01335 372289

Marshalls Mono Ltd
Brier Lodge, South Owrem,
Halifax, West Yorkshire
HX3 9SY
01422 306300

TIMBER/DECKING

Decking
Ryall & Edwards Ltd
Green Lane Sawmills, Outwood,
Nr Redhill, Surrey RH1 5QP
01342 842288

BSW Timber plc
Holly House Industrial Estate,
Middlewich Road, Cranage,
Cheshire CW10 9LT
01606 839100
www.bsw.co.uk

International Timber
West Yard, Trafford Wharf Road,
Trafford Park, Manchester M17 1DJ
0161 848 2900

Decking advice
The Timber Decking Association,
PO Box 99, A1 Business Park,
Pontefract, West Yorkshire
WF11 0YY
01977 679812, fax 01977 671701

Fencing
Down to Earth Fencing
34 Highland Avenue, Dagenham,
Essex RM10 7AS
020 8593 8969

Fence-Tech Ltd
Lealan Garden Centre, Bridgenorth
Road, Shipley, Pattingham,
Wolverhampton WV6 7EZ
01902 701381

Railway sleepers
F Hird & Sons,
Old Barton Lane,
Armthorpe,
Doncaster DN3 3AB
01302 831339

London Underground Ltd
Transplant
0777 197 6109

Reclaimed floor boards
RBS Oak
Brandon Lane, Coventry CV3 3GW
01203 639338

Reclaimed wood
Ashwell Recycling
Wick Place Farm, Brentwood Road,
Bulthan, Essex RM14 3TL
01375 892576, fax 01375 892330

Telegraph poles
Romsey Reclamation
The Old Goods Yard, Romsey
Railway Station, Romsey,
Hampshire SO51 8DU
01794 524174, fax 01794 514344

East Midlands Electricity (a division
of Powergen Energy plc)
www.eme.co.uk

Timber
Garrett Timber
Units 2 & 3, 54 Kimber Road,
London SW18 4PP
020 8877 1177

Geo. Hanson & Sons (Hucknall) Ltd
13 Watnall Road, Hucknall,
Nottinghamshire NG15 7LD
0115 963 2013

Gilmour & Aitkin Ltd Timber
Merchants
Milton Sawmills, Auchincarroch
Road, Jamestown, Alexandria,
Dunbartonshire G83 9EY
01389 752333

Goodwin and Company Artisans
Industrial Services Ltd
Unit 3a, Bruce Grove, Wickford,
Essex SS11 8BZ
01268 732250

James Latham Western
Badminton Road Trading Estate,
Yate, Bristol BS17 5JX
01454 315421

Nixon Knowles & Co Ltd
Longwall Avenue,
Queens Drive Industrial Estate,
Nottingham NG2 1LP
0115 986 5252, fax 0115 986 2198

Wood care products
Cuprinol Ltd
Adderwell, Frome,
Somerset BA11 1NL
01373 475000

PAINT

Dulux Exterior Paint
01753 691690

The Paint Centre
Unit 3, No. 1 Horton Close, West
Drayton, Middlesex UB7 8EB
01895 446232

TILES

Langleys
47–51 Great Suffolk Street,
London SE1 0FR
020 7803 4444

The Tile Association
020 8663 0946

The Tile Warehouse
131 Derby Road, Stapleford,
Nottingham NG9 7AS
0115 939 0209

LAWNS

Rolawn
Elvington, York YO41 4XR
01904 608661
info@rolawn-turf.co.uk

Rowlinson Garden Products
Crewe Gates Industrial Estate,
Weston Road, Crewe,
Cheshire CW1 6FJ
01270 506900
www.rowgar.co.uk

Turf Management Systems
Dromenagh Farm, Seven Hills
Road, Iver Heath,
Buckinghamshire SL0 0PA
01895 834411

PLANTS

Anglo Aquarium Plant Co Ltd
Strayfield Road, Enfield,
Middlesex EN2 9JE
020 8363 8548

Architectural Plants
Nuthurst, Horsham,
West Sussex RH13 6LH
01403 891772

Ausfern Nurseries at Kinglea
Plants Ltd
Sedge Green, Nazeing,
Essex EN9 2PA
01992 465073, fax 01992 465074
ausfern@attglobal.net

Civic Tree Care Ltd
Forestry House, PO Box 23,
Tring, Hertfordshire HP23 4AE
01442 825401
info@civictrees.co.uk,
www.civictrees.co.uk

Jungle Giants
Burford House Gardens,
Tenbury Wells, Worcestershire
WR15 8HQ
01584 819885

Mattocks Roses
0345 585652

Mimmacks Aquatics
Woodholne Nursery,
Goatsmoor Lane, Stock,
Essex CM4 9RS
01277 840204, fax 01277 841143

Mulu Nurseries
Burford House, Tenbury Wells,
Worcestershire WR15 8HQ
01584 811592, fax 01584 819301

Nottcutts Garden Centre
Ipswich Road, Woodbridge,
Suffolk IP12 4AF
01394 383344, fax 01394 445440

Tendercare
20 Southlands Road, Denham,
Uxbridge, Middlesex UB9 4HD
01895 835544

Wyevale Garden Centre
Headstone Lane, Harrow,
Middlesex HA2 6NB
0800 413213

*Greenhouse plants and
fruit trees*
The Van Hage Garden Company
Great Amwell, Nr Ware,
Hertfordshire SG12 9RP
01920 870811

Mature plants
Evergreen Exterior Services
21 Croydon Lane,
Banstead, Surrey SM7 3BW
020 8770 9200

FURNITURE

Café chairs
Debenhams
0845 609 9099
www.debenhams.com

Garden furniture
Konst Smide UK Ltd
Hardwick View Road, Holmewood
Industrial Estate, Holmewood,
Chesterfield, Derbyshire S42 5SA
01246 852140, fax 01246 854297

Rusty iron wigwam (mail order)
Room in the Garden
Oak Cottage, Furzen Lane, Ellens
Green, Rudgwick, West Sussex
RH12 3AR
01403 823958

Seat and serpent benches
Factory Furniture
The Stable Yard, Coleshill, Swindon
SN6 7PT
01793 763829

Spaceship
Advanced Mouldings
17 Benfield Way, Portslade,
Brighton BN41 2DA
01273 389465

LIGHTING

Caradon MK Electric Ltd
The Arnold Centre, Paycocke Road,
Basildon, Essex SS14 3EA
01268 563000, fax 01268 563563

Gardenlight Company
124a Bognor Road, Chichester,
West Sussex PO19 2NH
01243 787673, fax 01243 787673
will@onewithnature.freeserve.co.uk
www.gardenlightco.com

Lee Filters
Central Way, Walworth Industrial
Estate, Andover, Hampshire
SP10 6AN
01264 366245, fax 01264 355058
sales@leefilters.com
www.leefilters.com

Ring Lighting
Gelderd Road, Leeds LS12 6NB
0113 276 7676, fax 0113 263 8708

The Wholesale Lighting and
Electrical Company
34–41 White Lion Street,
London N1 9PQ
020 7278 8993

Neon lighting
AC/DC
Pasture Lane Works, Barrowford,
Nelson, Lancashire BB9 6ES
01282 601464

*Outdoor lighting and Christmas
lights*
Konst Smide UK Ltd
Hardwick View Road, Holmewood
Industrial Estate, Holmewood,
Chesterfield, Derbyshire S42 5SA
01246 852140, fax 01246 854297

WATER

Egmont Water Garden Centre
132 Tolworth Rise South, Surbiton,
Surrey KT5 9NJ
020 8337 9605

Hozelock Ltd
Waterslade House, Thame Road,
Haddenham, Aylesbury,
Buckinghamshire HP17 8JD
01844 292836

Lurgi Invent Ltd
Dell Road, Shawclough, Rochdale,
Lancashire OL12 6BZ
01706 359155, fax 01706 525271

Oase (UK) Ltd
2 North Way,
Walworth Industrial Estate,
Andover, Hampshire SP10 5OZ
01264 333225

Triton Chemical Manufacturing
Co Ltd
Triton House, Lyndean Industrial
Estate, 129 Felixstowe Road,
Abbeywood, London SE2 9SG
020 8310 3929, fax 020 8312 0349
www.triton-chemical.com

Butyl liner
Pond Liners Direct
Unit 4, Meridian Building, Nazeing
Glassworks, Nazeing New Road,
Broxbourne, Hertfordshire
EN10 6SX
01992 467053
www.pond-liners-pumps-
filters.co.uk
sales@pld.broxbourne.co.uk

Irrigation system
Landscape Watering Systems Ltd,
Bratch Lane, Dinton, Salisbury,
Wiltshire SP3 5EB
01722 716969

Water pumps
Lotus Water Garden Products
Second Floor Office Suite, Lodge
House, Lodge Square, Burnley
Lancashire BB11 1NW
01282 420771, fax 01282 412719

Water storage system and planters
Harcostar Drum Ltd
Windover Road, Huntingdon,
Cambridgeshire PE29 7EE
01480 52323

SOIL

Bailey's of Norfolk
Brick Kiln Road, Hevingham,
Norwich, Norfolk NR10 5NL
01603 754607, fax 01603 754147

Charles Morris Fertilizers Ltd
Longford House, Long Lane,
Stanwell, Middlesex TW19 7AT
01784 449144, fax 01784 449133

Woodland Horticultural Products
14 Woodborough Road, Winscombe,
Somerset BS25 1AD
01934 842906

*Bark mulches and natural play
surfaces*
Lyndcrest Ltd
Coven Heath Nursery, Shaw Hall
Lane, Coven Heath, Wolverhampton
WV10 7HE
01902 784478, fax 01902 784478

Melcourt Industries Ltd
Eight Bells House, Tetbury,
Gloucestershire GL8 8JG
01666 503919

Cocopeat
Wessex Horticultural Products Ltd
Wessex House, Units 1–3,
Hilltop Business Park, Devizes
Road, Salisbury, Wiltshire
SP3 4UF
01722 337744

Feeder system
PBI Home and Garden Ltd
1 Martin Bridge Trading Estate,
Lincoln Road, Enfield,
Middlesex EN1 1SP
020 8344 6808

MISCELLANEOUS

*Aquamac liquid membrane for
waterproofing trays*
Laybond Products Ltd
Riverside, Saltney, Chester
CH4 8RS
01244 674774

BBQ combination cooker
Morsø Multifuel and Gas Stoves
Wood Lane, Erdington,
Birmingham B24 9QP
0121 386 6306
www.morsostoves.co.uk

Nipooria UK Ltd
85b Main Road, Romford, Essex
RM2 5EL
01708 729123

Fiesta outdoor heaters
Sovereign Distributors UK Ltd
020 8386 5122, fax 020 8386 5123
sales@fiesta-heaters.com

Flues for stove
Selkirk Manufacturing Ltd
Pottington Industrial Estate,
Barnstaple, Devon EX31 1LZ
01271 326633, fax 01271 334303
www.selkirk.co.uk
info@selkirk.co.uk

Tower Ceramics
91 Parkway, London NW1 7PP
020 7251 6959

Galvanized planters
McVeigh Parker Southerns
Bradfield, Nr Reading, Berkshire
RG7 6HA
0118 974 4777 fax 0118 974 4123
www.mcveighparker.co.uk

Hammocks
Norfolk Leisure Company
Garage Lane, Setchey, King's Lynn,
Norfolk PE33 0BD
01553 811717, fax 01553 811818

Pulley system for drawbridge
Harold Potter Ltd
Daleside Road,
Nottingham, NG2 4DH
0115 986 6417

Roof canopy, external awnings
Mason Contract Ltd
17 High Street, Wallheath, King
Swinford, West Midlands DY6 0HB
01384 402800, fax 01384 402900

Slide
Early Learning Centre
08705 352352

Stone balls
Haddenstone Ltd
The Forge House, Church Lane,
East Haddon, Northamptonshire
NN6 8DB
01604 770711

Transfer of images to any surface
Lazertran Ltd
8 Alban Square, Aberaeron,
Ceredigion SA46 0AD
01545 571149
www.lazertran.com

PICTURE CREDIT

The photograph on
pp.134-5 was taken in
Petherton Road,
London N5.
Garden Design: Declan Buckley

INDEX